Colorful Vintage
Kitchen Towels

Erin Henderson & Yvonne Barineau

Photography by David DeHoyos
Assisted by Yvonne Barineau

Schiffer Publishing Ltd
4880 Lower Valley Road, Atglen, PA 19310 USA

Dedications

This book is wholeheartedly dedicated to my precious family, who are the ultimate loves of my life, and to our Father in heaven, through whom all things are possible.

—Yvonne Barineau

I dedicate this book to my husband Joe. Thank you for your encouragement and love.

—Erin Henderson

Copyright © 2006 by Erin Henderson and Yvonne Barineau
Library of Congress Control Number: 2005938938

All rights reserved. No part of this work may be reproduced or used in any form or by any means—graphic, electronic, or mechanical, including photocopying or information storage and retrieval systems—without written permission from the publisher.
The scanning, uploading and distribution of this book or any part thereof via the Internet or via any other means without the permission of the publisher is illegal and punishable by law. Please purchase only authorized editions and do not participate in or encourage the electronic piracy of copyrighted materials.
"Schiffer," "Schiffer Publishing Ltd. & Design," and the "Design of pen and ink well" are registered trademarks of Schiffer Publishing Ltd.

Designed by John P. Cheek
Type set in Bernhard Modern BT/Korinna BT

ISBN: 0-7643-2380-6
Printed in China
1 2 3 4

Published by Schiffer Publishing Ltd.
4880 Lower Valley Road
Atglen, PA 19310
Phone: (610) 593-1777; Fax: (610) 593-2002
E-mail: Info@schifferbooks.com

For the largest selection of fine reference books on this and related subjects, please visit our web site at
www.schifferbooks.com
We are always looking for people to write books on new and related subjects. If you have an idea for a book please contact us at the above address.

This book may be purchased from the publisher.
Include $3.95 for shipping.
Please try your bookstore first.
You may write for a free catalog.

In Europe, Schiffer books are distributed by
Bushwood Books
6 Marksbury Ave.
Kew Gardens
Surrey TW9 4JF England
Phone: 44 (0) 20 8392-8585;
Fax: 44 (0) 20 8392-9876
E-mail: info@bushwoodbooks.co.uk
Website: www.bushwoodbooks.co.uk
Free postage in the U.K., Europe; air mail at cost.

Contents

Acknowledgments 4
Introduction 5
Chapter 1. How Does Your Garden Grow? 6
Chapter 2. Hand Work 28
Chapter 3. Songs of the South: Western, Black Americana, South of the Rio Grande 36
Chapter 4. Happy Couples and Funny Faces 47
Chapter 5. Cocktails Anyone? 71
Chapter 6. Sets and Stripes 76
Chapter 7. Designers 84
Chapter 8. Animals 100
Chapter 9. Conversational 107
Acquisition, Cleaning, and Storage 131
Manufacturers 135
Glossary of Textile Terms 153
Resource Guide 156
Bibliography 158
Index 159

Acknowledgments

Without the help of some dear folks, this book would not have been possible. We wish to thank our patient families for tolerating our piles of vintage towels and accessories. Thanks to Auntie Margaret for her inspiration and love and to Sandra McNichol and Diane Fifer for their unconditional friendship and unending support. Immeasurable love to Jerry and Jeannine McKain and Bill and Stephanie Barineau for a faith that could move mountains.

Our gratitude goes to Tamara Bogdanovich and Helena Jones for sharing their personal memories of artists Tamara and Sergei Bogdanovich and to Carol Bailey of the Putnam County Historical Society for her research efforts. Thanks also to the Kay Dee Company for sharing their history with us and to Dever Larmor of Ulster Linen Co., Inc. We are grateful to designer Martin Ryan for taking the time via phone and e-mail to share his fascinating stories with us.

Thanks to Sharon Stark, Lynette Gray, Donna Cardwell, Deborah Payne, Michelle Hayes, and Dr. Christine Dickinson for loaning a few pieces of their vast collection and to Leslie Upson for the neat tidbit of information she shared with us. Thanks to Lynda Saxton for her humor, honesty, and "woo-hoo-hoos." Once again, we must thank our very sweet editor, Donna Baker, for patiently letting us pester her with questions. Kudos to David "MacGyver" DeHoyos, whose photography talent we appreciate more than ever. We are grateful to Yvonne's favorite quilting shop, Quakertown Quilts in Friendswood, Texas, for allowing us to invade their store on a busy Saturday morning to take pictures.

A *very* special thanks to the owners of Butler's Courtyard in League City, Texas for opening the doors of their incredible special events facility to us. Many of the decorative photographs in the book were taken in their beautifully furnished historical buildings, and for that we are indebted.

Introduction

They are called by a multitude of names: tea towels, dish towels, kitchen towels, utility towels, bar towels, work towels, and hand towels. They come in a multitude of fibers: linen, cotton, crash linen, Wonder Dri, Dry Me Dry. Their styles vary wildly from whimsical, floral, fruity, and risqué, to downright elegant. With so many variables involved in these vintage towels, it is no wonder collectors can't seem to get enough of them!

We have noticed a marked rise in popularity of this previously overlooked vintage textile in recent years. Being obsessed collectors ourselves, it is easy to understand why these items are finally getting the attention they deserve. Vintage towels are small art canvases ~ easily afforded, easily cleaned, and easily displayed. In contrast to their unwieldy (but beloved) tablecloth cousins, hundreds of different designs can be tucked away in a fraction of the space and at a fraction of the cost.

Part of our fascination with these colorful canvases is with the artists themselves. Largely unknown Masters designed exquisite explosions of colors, which were then hand printed onto a variety of fabrics. While some designers signed their work, most of the artists' names will never be known. Even with access to billions of pieces of data on the Internet, sometimes information about these brilliant artists simply isn't available. The "designer" towels often command greater prices simply because of their signatures, yet many of our favorites will pass into perpetuity as mysteries. Be sure to read about the talented design team for the Wilendur company, Tamara and Sergei Bogdanovich (see page 98) ~ to the best of our knowledge, their interesting stories have not been publicly known to collectors until now.

The values assigned in this book are based on a variety of sources; we have diligently searched antique stores, flea markets, estate sales, and reputable Internet dealers. Nearly every piece in this book is in mint, unused condition and the prices are adjusted upward accordingly. The value of a faded, stained, or damaged towel will be significantly lower than priced here ~ often as much as 80% less.

We hope this book inspires you to either *begin* a new vintage towel collection or add to your current one. If nothing else, we hope you take away an appreciation of the art of textile design. Welcome to our obsession!

For many collectors, the appeal of colorful kitchen towels can be summed up in this vintage print and poem. While most women in the 21st century don't "toil the precious hours away" in the kitchen, the warmth and nostalgia of the vintage kitchen holds an endearing appeal ~ it was a place where there were warm cookies waiting after school, the scent of pot roast wafted through open windows, and where the family *always* met for meals and laughter. *Vintage poem and print copyright the Buzza Company, MPLS USA. From the collection of Deborah Payne.*

Chapter 1
How Does Your Garden Grow?

Unfailingly cheerful yardage of Wilendur Shasta Daisy fabric for use in making towels, runners, curtains, and other kitchen accessories. This design can be found in a wide array of colors including blue, green, red, yellow, brown, and burgundy. 18 inches selvedge width. *Photo taken at Butler's Courtyard, League City, Texas.*
Price Range: $35-$45 per yard

Sunny yellow and snowy white blossoms are splashed across heavy weight cotton sailcloth. This vintage towel by Wilendur is called Verbena and also came in red, purple, pink, and blue. Tales of verbena have been recorded for centuries. Ancient civilization credited the plant with medicinal attributes, from treating rheumatism to aiding digestion. (Don't try this at home!) The Romans, always concerned about romance, named verbena "Plant of Venus" (after the goddess of love and beauty) and believed it would rekindle the flames of dying passion. To modern civilization, the verbena is simply one of the showiest of all nature's perennial flowers, and it has never been depicted more beautifully than on this towel.
Measurements: 17x33 inches
Price Range: $30-$35

A vivid display of orange-red poppies and blue ribbons on this Technicolor Print towel of sateen and cotton. The design is incredibly realistic ~ an advanced printing technique for the era. The tag states that the towel is absorbent and lintless, and instructs us to wash it with pure soap in lukewarm water and not to rub. If you look closely, you can see the word "Eaton" printed in the border. This is one of three Technicolor Print patterns in our collections, all with Eaton printed within their border design. The original Eaton store price sticker is still affixed to the towel. Eaton's Department Stores were a Canadian institution for over 125 years, operating from 1869-1999. "Goods Satisfactory or Money Refunded" was their slogan. Timothy Eaton (1834-1907) opened his first department store in Toronto in 1869 and in 1884 he started a Canada-wide mail-order catalog service that came to be known as the "Homesteader's Bible." *Photo taken at Butler's Courtyard, League City, Texas.*
Measurements: 17x29 inches
Price Range: $30-35

Broderie Creations is known among collectors for their whimsical prints of people and animals, but this one defies the norm with dainty, elegant gardenias on a creamy linen background.
Measurements: 15x29 inches
Price Range: $25-$30

A cheerful spring tulip design by Cannon, with its original manufacturer sticker and W.T. Grant Department Store tags attached. At only .15 cents per towel, this would have been an affordable way to brighten the kitchen.
Measurements: 16x33 inches
Price Range: $25-$30

The color is intoxicating and the design remarkably realistic on this poppy towel by GW Textile Product ~ a brilliant explosion of color on satiny cotton sailcloth. The poppy is known throughout the world as a symbol of remembrance to honorable soldiers who sacrificed their lives for freedom. Colonel John McCrae, a distinguished medical officer in World War I, wrote *In Flanders Fields* on a page torn from his dispatch book. This heartfelt poem inspired numerous other poets to pen and publish similar poetic responses, vowing "never to forget" the powerful symbol of the poppies of Flanders.

> In Flanders' fields the poppies blow
> Between the crosses, row on row
> That mark our place, and in the sky
> The larks still bravely singing, fly
> Scarce heard amid the guns below.
> We are the dead, short days ago
> We lived, felt dawn, saw sunset glow.
> Loved, and were loved, and now we lie
> In Flanders' fields.
> Take up our quarrel with the foe,
> To you from failing hands we throw
> The Torch: be yours to hold it high!
> If ye break faith with us who die
> We shall not sleep, though poppies grow
> In Flanders' fields.

This towel is heavily soiled from storage and will require a gentle soak to remove sixty years of grime. Because Technicolor prints tend to fade in modern cleaning chemicals, a gentle Ivory Snow bath would be recommended.
Measurements: 16x26 inches
Price Range: $30-$35

Something a bit different ~ the decorative, factory applied crochet border is a delightful change from the normal hemmed edges of most print tea towels.
Measurements: 16x29 inches
Price Range: $25-$30

8

Full view of butterfly and dogwood towel

Butterflies and dogwood adorn this vivid red linen towel and a sweetly scalloped edge dresses up one side ~ the other three sides are hemmed. The Town & Country logo, a petite horse and buggy, can be found printed on one corner. *Photo taken at Butler's Courtyard, League City, Texas.*
Measurements 16x28 inches
Price Range: $25-$30

A lovely linen hand printed towel featuring stylized poppies and wildflowers by the manufacturer Stevens. The design repeats on both ends.
Measurements: 16x30 inches
Price Range: $20-$25

This Wilendur Butterfly Bush pattern is so realistically detailed, one can almost expect to see the dainty insects it was named for hovering near the blossoms! This beauty was designed by artists Tamara and Sergei Bogdanovich. Wilendur applied for a 3-1/2 year design patent on their behalf on March 23, 1956. It has a fringed edge rather than the standard Wilendur hem, a decorative innovation we've seen several times on other Wilendur patterns.
Measurements: 17x36 inches including fringe
Price Range: $30-$35

9

Realistic poppy and wildflower bouquets are the theme of this Startex cotton towel. The original .39 price sticker from The Leader Store in Hazelton, Pennsylvania is still affixed.
Measurements: 16x32 inches
Price Range: $20-$25

The Pride of Flanders, an early Wilendur company, used the finest Belgian linen in the manufacturing of their textiles. This one is lightweight and has a silky, luxurious feel ~ an elegant beauty that can be better appreciated when running the cloth between the fingertips.
Measurements: 14x21 inches
Price Range: $20-$25

A French blue grid forms the background for wild roses on this Lynbrook pattern towel by Wilendur. It also came in yellow, red, and two shades of green.
Measurements: 17x33 inches
Price Range: $30-$35

A dozen Wilendur floral towels flutter in the spring breeze. *Photo taken in the gardens of Butler's Courtyard, League City, Texas.*

Vines of sapphire blue clematis climb across this Wilendur towel of the same name. Clematis is a showy flowering vine that comes in thousands of varieties. There is an old saying about clematis that "the first year they sleep; the second year they creep; the third year they leap." This lovely towel came in a variety of colors including red, blue, and yellow.
Measurements: 17x33 inches
Price Range: $30-$35

An impressionistic floral design by The Pride of Flanders, hand printed on luxurious, light weight linen.
Measurements: 14x20 inches
Price Range: $20-$25

A profusion of purple violets adorn this heavy linen towel by Hardy Craft Originals. This Viola pattern was produced in an ensemble of kitchen pieces including tablecloths, aprons, and potholders. Note the overlocked (or serged) edges, rather than the more customary hemming.
Measurements: 16x32 inches
Price Range: $30-$35

Hardy Craft Viola tablecloth to complement the matching towel. This tablecloth was featured in our previous book, *Colorful Tablecloths 1930s-1960s: Threads of the Past.*

11

Ivy print toweling in rich tones of green and blue, sold by the yard to be made into towels, curtains, placemats, seat cushions, or whatever the imaginative housewife could come up with. *Photo taken at Butler's Courtyard, League City, Texas.*
Measurements: 16 inches selvedge width
Price Range: $35-$45 per yard

Just a touch of Mexican flair ~ a petite terra cotta pitcher is nestled underneath a colorful arrangement of violets on this Wilendur towel. Although Wilendur touted their towels as "absorbent and lintless," the heavy cotton sailcloth is a bit too dense to be absorbent. We find them more serviceable as table runners. They are, nevertheless, our favorite brand of vintage towels and are wildly popular with collectors.
Measurements: 17x30 inches
Price Range: $30-$35

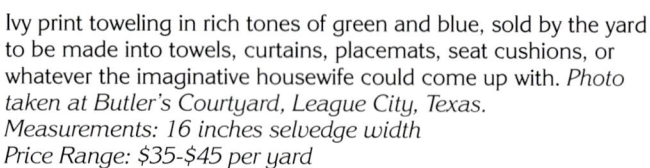

Large American Beauty roses are realistically displayed on each end of this towel, which also came in pink and yellow. While collectors often assume this is a Wilendur design because of its repeating pattern and heavy sailcloth, the only one we've seen to date with a paper tag has been by Lady Price, a mercantile company that began producing textiles for the home in 1953. Regardless of the maker, it is exquisite and worthy of any collector's cache.
Measurements: 18x35 inches
Price Range: $30-$35

Pretty blue thistle pop against a tartan plaid background. This Startex towel is a weave of 75% cotton and 25% linen and still retains its original Penny's price tag ~ at four for $1.00 they were an affordable addition to the vintage kitchen.
Measurements: 17x31 inches
Price Range: $25-$30

A springtime delight from Mastercraft Hand Prints. Note that the Mastercraft signature is printed on one corner of the cloth.
Measurements: 17x27 inches
Price Range: $25-$30

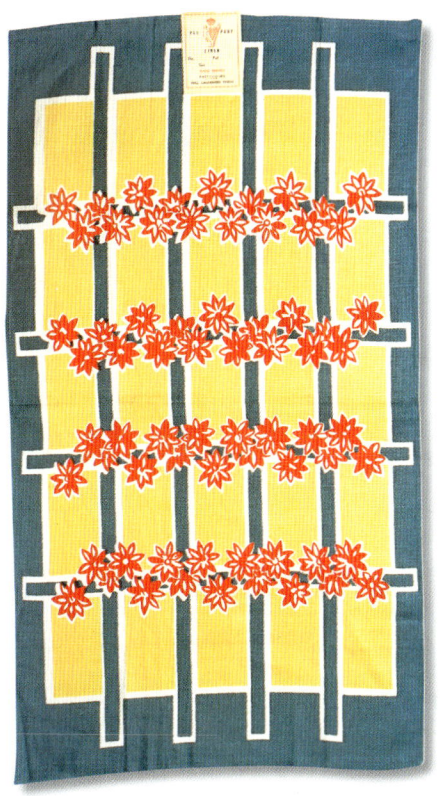

A vivid break from the typical floral towel! Although the original paper tag is still attached to this bold linen beauty, no manufacturer name is given.
Measurements: 17x31 inches
Price Range: $20-$35

Pick your favorite color ~ this "old store stock" trio of daisy towels is a cheerful delight! All linen with the original paper Leacock tags attached.
Measurements: 16x29 inches
Price Range: $30-$35

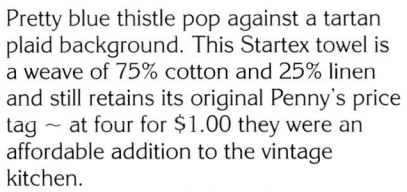

Full view of Wilendur floral towel.

Large and lovely enough to be a table runner, but the tag gives away its true calling as an "absorbent, lintless" Wilendur towel.
Measurements: 17x34 inches
Price Range: $30-$35

Look closely at these petite Pride of Flanders towels ~ the dense floral design hides young courting lovers and art deco deer. The fabric is fine, lightweight Belgian linen that would be equally serviceable in the powder room or draped across a tea tray. They are photographed with an old wooden spool from a mill room.
Measurements: 12x21 inches
Price Range: $20-$25

Trio of spun rayon and cotton towels by America's Pride. The pattern is exquisite and the colors *divine*, but the high rayon content keeps them from being absorbent. They would be better suited as decorative table runners or display towels.
Measurements: 17x29 inches
Price Range: $30-$35

Trio of Wilendur towels made of heavy cotton sailcloth.

Artist John Madsen was granted a design patent for this Rhododendron pattern on May 11, 1948. This beautiful towel came in blue, green, grey, and yellow.
Measurements 17x30 inches
Price Range: $30-$35

Cheerful polka dots surround a floral design on this two-color linen towel by Eye Appeal. The label states it is guaranteed fast color.
Measurements: 17x 30 inches
Price Range: $20-$25

15

Fabulous fall colors and a richly detailed design ~ another masterpiece by artists Tamara and Sergei Bogdanovich, circa May 24, 1955. When found in harvest colors, this Wilendur pattern is called Autumn; in green it is named Ivy.
Measurements: 17x34 inches
Price Range: $30-$35

Wilendur strikes again with a simplistic yet stunning design of yellow poppies on a creamy white background.
Measurements: 17x34 inches
Price Range: $30-$35

Wilendur towel in the Meadow pattern. *Photo taken at Butler's Courtyard, League City, Texas.*
Measurements: 17x34 inches
Price Range: $30-$35

A variety of cheerful flowers with berries scattered in to add interest. Another lovely pattern by Wilendur.
Measurements: 17x27 inches
Price Range: $30-$35

Exotic fuchsia blossoms drip from this pair of linen towels by California Hand Prints. CHP designed, printed, marketed, and distributed their line of towels, tablecloths, and beach wear from a shop located on Hermosa Beach. Local residents reminisced with us about walking into the front of the shop to buy beach towels while the printing process of other goods was taking place at the back of the building. Few CHP towels are found in the marketplace ~ their tablecloths are more readily available.
Measurements: 17x30 inches
Price Range: $30-$35

Few Wilendur patterns depicted animals ~ floral and fruit patterns were by far more common. While primarily floral, this unusual Wilendur towel features a zebra figurine against vivid red hibiscus blossoms. The bold used of fiesta colors make a colorful and cheerful towel.
Measurements: 17x27 inches
Price Range: $30-$35

A duo of Fruit of the Loom towels with the .59 cent price stickers from Hill Brothers Fashion Center. Like a favorite pair of well worn jeans, the colors are softly muted ~ not *faded*, but actually designed with an acid washed appearance. Be sure to see page 140 in the manufacturer section of this book for an interesting story about how the Fruit of the Loom name and logo were chosen.
Measurements: 15x29 inches
Price Range: $20-$25 each

Precious Broderie gardening gal with a basket of freshly cut flowers perched upon her head. This lovely lassie is printed on one end of the towel only ~ the other side shows only the garden fence. Heavy cotton sailcloth with the original paper tag attached.
Measurements: 17x28 inches
Price Range: $40-$45

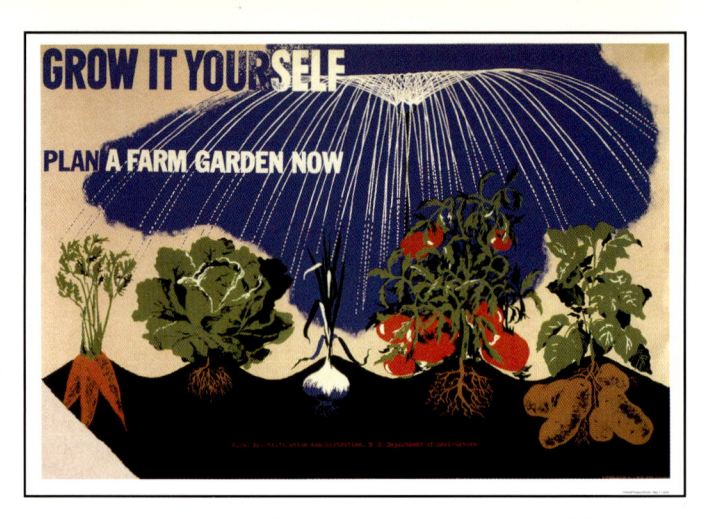

During World Wars I and II, patriotic Americans planted "Victory Gardens" in an effort to maintain a supply of fresh fruits and vegetables for civilians and troops. As described on the Smithsonian Institution's web site, a nationwide effort was put forth to make the gardens a success ~ government agencies, schools, businesses, and private foundations worked in conjunction with seed companies to provide communities with land and the necessary guidance for successfully maintaining their gardens. For many individuals, especially those in metropolitan areas, this was their first attempt at growing their own food. Magazine and newspaper articles helped to provide instruction and colorful posters such as this one from the U.S. Department of Agriculture encouraged folks to keep up the good work. Gardeners worked to harvest fresh food for family and neighbors during the summer months, with enough left over to can and preserve for winter-time consumption. Across the nation, young and old Americans proudly took part in transforming backyards, vacant lots, parks, and schoolyards into flourishing gardens. The effort was especially successful during WWII, as millions of gardens ~ ranging in size from window boxes to large fields ~ were planted and lovingly tended. Today we have only mementos of these once bountiful Victory Gardens ~ posters such as this one and vintage kitchen linens are especially colorful reminders of an era all Americans should be proud of.

Colorful 1940s cotton conversational towel featuring a lovely lady returning home from the flower market, her basket overflowing with posies and a bouquet tucked under one arm. We found it interesting that she seems to be in a big city, rather than a more typical rural scene.
Measurements: 15x28 inches
Price Range: $25-$30

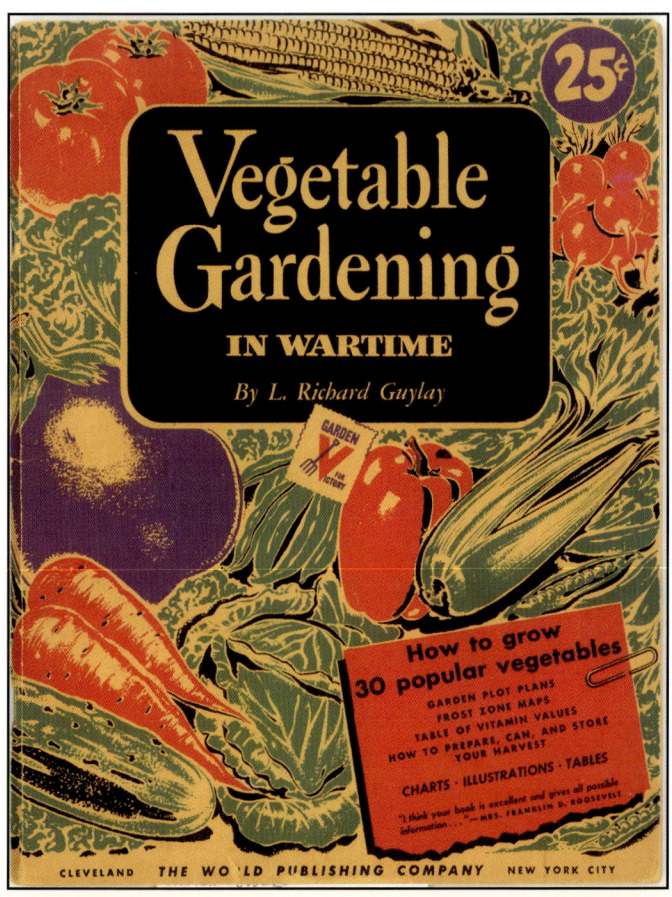

As noted above, World War II era Americans proclaimed their patriotism by cultivating victory gardens. This book, *Vegetable Gardening in Wartime* (copyright 1943 by The World Publishing Company, Cleveland and New York) is described as "The complete guide to a successful Victory Garden." Garden themed textiles were extremely popular during the World War II era, often depicting stylish women and attractive men toiling in the garden or selling their wares.

18

Get your fresh vegetables and fruits here! Close-up of a wonderful garden theme towel featuring a young farmer selling produce from his road side stand. It appears he had a bountiful harvest!
Measurements: 15x27 inches
Price Range: $25-$30

It's hard not to smile at this vegetable peddler with his cheerful outfit and comical handlebar moustache. The design is printed on one end of the towel only.
Measurements: 17x28 inches
Price Range: $25-$30

Beautiful women were often depicted on World War II era gardening towels ~ perhaps motivation for the housewife to maintain her *own* victory garden? Funny, though, that they never seemed to get their hands dirty!
Measurements: 15x26 inches
Price Range: $30-$35

This lovely lassie seems more dressed for a party than work in her victory garden.
Measurements: 15x28 inches
Price Range: $30-$35

Now *this* beautiful young woman is dressed to work, wearing bib overalls, a straw hat, and heavy work gloves. It looks like she has a bumper crop of turnips this year, which she's managing to harvest without getting a single hair out of place! The towel is made from very heavy cotton. Notice the heavy over-dying of colors to add shade and depth to the design ~ a classic 1930s-1940s print technique.
Measurements: 16x28 inches
Price Range: $30-$35

A lovely young lady in high heeled shoes, a colorful dress, and Betty Grable styled hair appears to have finished working in the garden and is now dressed for market.
Measurements: 17x30 inches
Price Range: $30-$35

Look closely at this design…what may appear at first glance to be a pear, an apple, and a pepper hides a busy farmer working in the garden. A simple, eye-catching pattern in bold red on creamy linen.
Measurements: 16x29 inches
Price Range: $25-$30

From the maker Victory K&B, this linen towel features a geometric design of carrots, peppers, and peas. The combination of color, style, and overprinting all point to a World War II era birth date.
Measurements: 16x32 inches
Price Range: $20-$25

Fruit themed linen towel with bold colors by The Pride of Flanders. Notice the overprinting of colors, a classic technique of the 1930s and 1940s. This towel is made from the high quality Belgian linen Weil and Durrse offered on *all* their Pride of Flanders products.
Measurements: 17x31 inches
Price Range: $30-$35

California Hand Prints strawberry towel of extremely heavy cotton sailcloth.
Measurements: 16x28 inches
Price Range: $30-$35

Veggie delight by The Pride of Flanders. These pure linen towels are little works of art, designed by John Madsen in 1939. One features turnips, radishes, peas, and peppers and a border of runner beans; the other two boast plump ripe red tomatoes, eggplant, corn, and cucumbers with a border of radishes. Both patterns came in all primary colors: blue, red, green, and yellow. In our experience, these towels hold their vivid color quite well with proper washing, making them a joy to put to gentle use in the kitchen.
Measurements: 17x30 inches
Price Range: $35-45

This fruit towel by GW boasts an advanced use of color and printing for the era, utilizing a process called Litho Craft. The detailed design appears to be lifted off a painting canvas and placed directly onto the towel. *Photo taken at Butler's Courtyard, League City, Texas.*
Measurements: 16x27 inches
Price Range: $30-$35

Full view of GW Litho Craft fruit towel. Towels by this manufacturer are some of the most extraordinarily realistic designs we have seen and are worthy of any collection. We must warn you to use caution when washing textiles that utilized "Litho Craft" or "Technicolor" techniques, as we've found modern cleaning chemicals can drastically fade the design. A gentle soak in Liquid Ivory Snow is a safe alternative. We think the extra effort is a great trade-off for such spectacular color!
Measurements: 16x27 inches
Price Range: $30-$35

An orderly row of blue cherries frames this fruity towel by Broderie Creations. A lovely design on natural linen.
Measurements: 15x28 inches
Price Range: $30-$35

All three of these mouthwateringly realistic towels share the same name: *Strawberry*. The center towel is by Leacock and the outside duo are Wilendur(e) patterns. John Madsen designed the pattern on the far right and applied for a design patent on January 19, 1944. The Leacock towel can be found in the 1943 Montgomery Ward catalog, priced at .74 cents each, or 2/$1.39 with color choices of blue, green, or red.
Measurements: Wilendurs, 17x33 inches; Leacock, 16x29 inches
Price Range: $30-$35 each

An orchard of stylized fruit decorates this Leda print, appropriately named "Fruit." Use caution when washing this cloth, as we have found it to have unstable fugitive dyes that can fade rapidly in the first wash. Once the first wash is complete, the color tends to remain stable. We found this pattern in the 1943 Montgomery Ward catalog for an affordable .28 cents each, or 4/$1.
Measurements: 16x28 inches
Price Range: $20-$25

Startex Mills strawberry towel of 75% cotton and 25% linen.
Measurements: 16x31 inches
Price Range: $20-$25

25

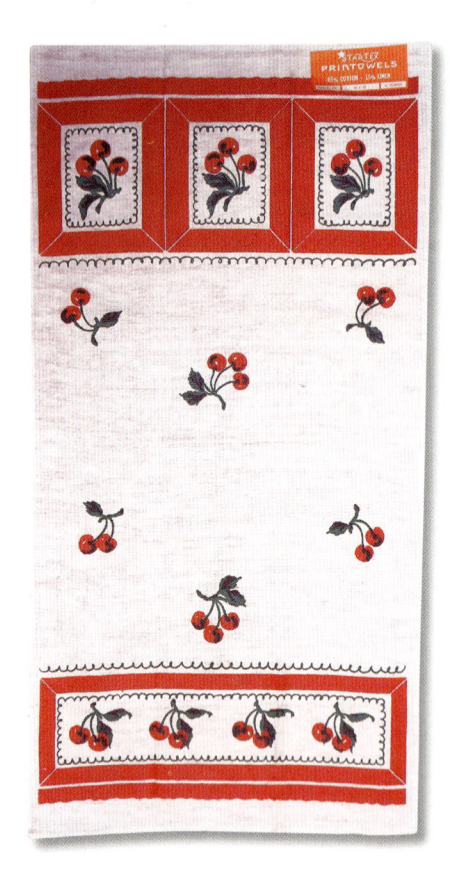

Startex cherry towel. These towels were often packaged in factory bundles of six or twelve, which could be broken apart at the discretion of the store owner for individual resale.
Measurements: 16x33 inches
Price Range: $20-$25

At first glance, this yardage of toweling appears to be the classic Wilendur(e) Strawberry pattern, but several inconsistencies in the design betray it as an imposter: the fabric is coarse and grainy, the colors are not as rich, and it is missing the telltale blossoms of the Wilendur(e) pattern. As with most yardage of vintage toweling, the manufacturer of this fabric is unknown. Width is 17 inches from side hem to side hem. *Photo taken at Butler's Courtyard, League City, Texas.*
Price Range: $25-$30 per yard

Trio of Wilendur apple and fruit towels designed by artist John S. Madsen, who applied for a 3-1/2 year design patent on March 22, 1940. This pattern came in every primary color ~ blue, red, yellow, and green. The original 5/$1.00 price tag from Cleland Simpson Company in Scranton, Pennsylvania is still attached. *Photo taken at Butler's Courtyard, League City, Texas.*
Measurements: 17x29 inches
Price Range: $30-$35

A bountiful harvest of fresh vegetables is found on this vintage toweling of heavy cotton sailcloth. Rather than selvedge edges, the long sides are hemmed and measure 16-1/2 inches across. *Photo taken at Butler's Courtyard, League City, Texas.*
Price Range: $25-$30 per yard

A cheerful strawberry print by Leacock in pure, absorbent linen. *Photo taken at Butler's Courtyard, League City, Texas.*
Measurements: 16x29 inches
Price Range: $25-$30

Chapter 2
Hand Work

Close-up of hand work on the huck woven towel below.

A duo of charming blue birds adorn this huck (short for huckabuck) towel. Huck woven towels are made of a pebbly textured cloth that offers both absorbency and long wear. A relatively simple method of decorating the cloth is called Swedish embroidery, or huck weaving. This was an extremely popular technique in the 1930s and 1940s, and, in spite of its name, the art form is thought to have originated in Denmark rather than Sweden. Using this method, the colorful thread is merely slipped under the loops of the huck fabric, rather than stitching all the way through. If properly executed, the design will be visible only on the top of the fabric and not from the back side. Blue birds were, and still are, a very popular collectible theme, and such superior workmanship will add to the value of this towel.
Measurements: 17x29 inches
Price Range: $25-$30

Swedish embroidery huck towels with *exceptionally* fine crochet edges. Because of the spectacular handwork and delightful candy colors, the value of these three are higher than more common huck weave towels. *Photo taken at Butler's Courtyard, League City, Texas.* Price Range: $35-$40 each

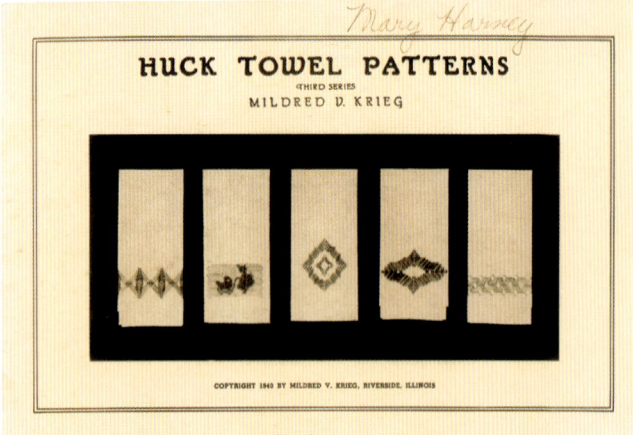

Huck Towel Patterns, copyright 1936 and 1940 by Mildred V. Krieg, Riverside, Illinois.

A fun find! The tag on this anthropomorphic towel identifies it as a store display ~ no doubt to show crafters what the finished product would look like. The needle art company, Lorraine, was in business since 1888.
Measurements: 16x25
Price Range: $20-$25

Close-up of colorful hand embroidery towel ~ a pitcher of water and basket of flowers perched upon a wooden foot stool.
Measurements: 18x25 inches
Price Range: $15-$20

This chubby chef seems to be enjoying his own cooking a bit too much! Hand embroidered and appliquéd towel by Paragon.
Measurements: 17x28 inches
Price Range: $20-$25

Not all hand made towels were "home" made. This delightful duo was hand appliquéd and embroidered by Paragon and sold as a boxed set. One towel features a chef proudly displaying his latest masterpiece, a turkey. The other showcases a maid carrying a tray with a whimsical teapot and cup. There is some storage soiling on the pair, which should be easy to remove by utilizing the cleaning suggestions in the back of this book.
Measurements: 18x29 inches
Price range: $50-$60 pair

Two decorative books containing assorted size needles to complete any hand work project.

"God Bless Our Home" ~ a pristine pair of towels featuring hand appliquéd and embroidery work. The gentleman is eagerly awaiting the casserole his lovely wife has prepared for him. These towels were once display "models" used by Dayton's Department store to sell kits. Later (most likely when the kit was discontinued), the models were priced to sell in their finished form. The original $5 price was marked down to $2.50 for the pair.
Measurements: 16x27 inches
Price Range: $50-$60 pair

Charming family portraits of hubby and wife by Bucilla Needlecraft. It was fun to find the washing instructions still included with the set: *"We recommend Lux Flakes; do not roll or fold while wet; embroidered pieces should be dried flat on a table or hung up. Iron on reverse side after thoroughly dry."*
Measurements: 18x24 inches
Price Range: $50-$60 pair

31

These three charming towels date to the World War II era and feature lovely ladies in various dress of the period, appliquéd onto cotton flour sack with embroidery accents. The blind appliqué stitches are absolutely, perfectly even ~ superb hand work.
Price Range: $45-$50 set

A demur señorita drops a rose over the balcony to her lover below. These hand appliquéd and embroidered linen towels were produced by Progress (Tobin, Sporn, and Glaser) and are exceptionally detailed.
Measurements: 17x26 inches
Price Range: $50-$60 pair

Playful puppy days-of-the-week towel set made of vintage flour sack. While it is often difficult to discern whether embroidered towels are truly vintage or recent re-creations, occasionally there are dead giveaways. True flour sack towels will often have a row of tiny pinprick holes along one edge where the drawstring closure of the sack was removed. Vintage flour sack will not have a sewn-in label of any kind. Finding a complete set that is truly vintage is becoming harder, and the value is reflected accordingly.
Price Range: $95-$125

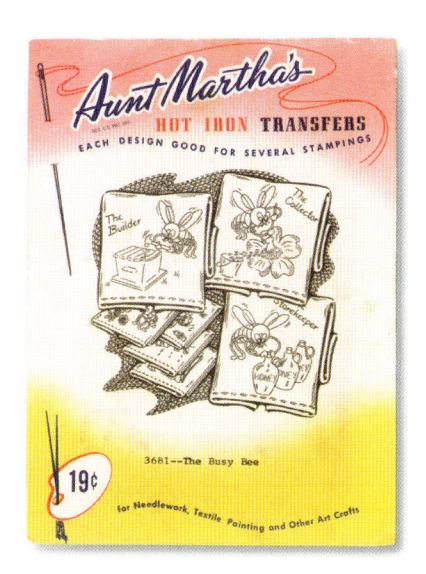

Aunt Martha and Vogart transfer patterns for needlework, textile painting, and other crafts.

Adorable Sunbonnet Sue days-of-the-week towels, expertly hand embroidered onto absorbent cotton muslin. This set was recently re-created from a vintage pattern ~ a true vintage set would be worth *at least* twice as much. It can be difficult to tell the difference between old and new without relying on the honesty and expertise of a reputable textile dealer. Regardless of the age, a collector would be thrilled to own handwork of this quality.
Price Range: $45-$50 new or $95-$125 vintage

A set of kitten days-of-the-week towels, recently stitched from a vintage pattern. As complete sets of vintage embroidered towels become more difficult to find, reusing old patterns on new towels has become an increasingly popular option ~ collectors can use and abuse them without the guilt sometimes associated with damaging vintage items. This cute set has been recently embroidered; if vintage, the price could easily double or triple. *From the collection of Donna Cardwell (www.dcardblueslinencloset.com).*
Price Range: $45-$50 new or $95-$125 vintage

33

Since the beginning of time, mankind has been fascinated with space and dreamed of soaring into the stars and exploring the planets. This dream became a reality with the NASA Apollo program. From the devastating pre-launch fire of Apollo 1 on January 27, 1967 that killed all three astronauts on board, to the resounding success of the Apollo 11 moon landing on July 20, 1969, people the world over have been enamored with space flight. These adorable hand appliquéd and embroidered towels are a testament to the fascination Americans had with the Apollo program. From a child's eye view, the various stages of space flight are recorded: Countdown, In Orbit, Space Walk, Splashdown, and Pick Up. To a younger generation familiar only with space shuttle flights, "Splashdown" and "Pick Up" may be foreign terms. Without modern shuttle landing technology, space capsules would literally "splash down" into the ocean, their decent into the earth's atmosphere slowed by massive parachutes. Fleets of Naval aircraft carriers, boats, and teams of divers would be waiting nearby for "pick up." The astronauts would climb safely from the capsule and the flight would be a success. The last splash down of a manned rocket was the Apollo-Soyuz Test Project in 1975, so these towels were likely created prior to that date. We suspect they were made at the height of the United States and USSR space race in the late 1960s, and we've never seen another set comparable: the design is charming and the hand work is exceptionally superior.
Price Range: $95-$125

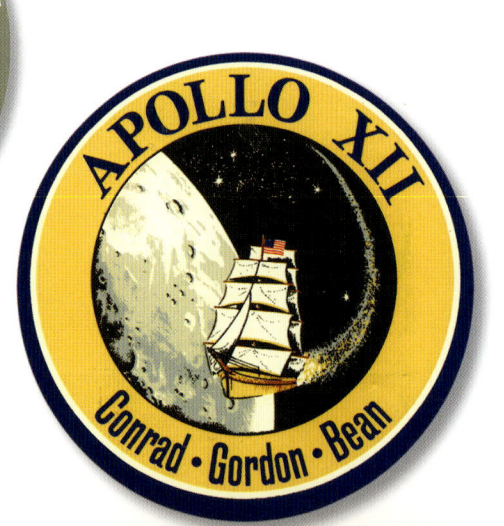

These commemorative NASA stickers are examples of those given to employees as tokens of appreciation for their work and dedication to the space program.

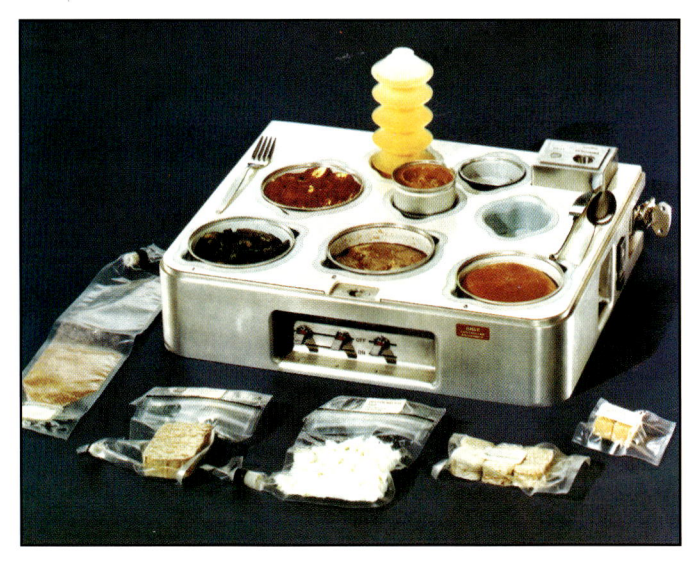

Food for a space flight is shown in this NASA photo from the 1970s. Where's their vintage towel???

Another NASA photo shows the famous descent leading to "one small step for man, one giant leap for mankind."

We couldn't resist showing off Yvonne's father, Gerald McKain (left), accepting an award for his service at NASA.

Beautifully hand embroidered and appliquéd lemon and orange tree towels. These were sold as kits to be finished at home.
Measurements: 17x26 inches
Price Range: $45-$50 set

35

Chapter 3

Songs of the South: Western, Black Americana, South of the Rio Grande

1950s Startex cowboy-western themed towel that matches a tablecloth and napkin set. Unlike its tablecloth cousin, the towel is a linen/cotton blend, rather than all cotton. We think The Duke approves! *Photo taken at Butler's Courtyard, League City, Texas.*
Measurements: 16x31 inches
Price Range: $50-$55

Full view of Startex cowboy towel.

A fabulous find! This cowboy-western themed Startex tablecloth was found in its original box and matches the towel on previous page. Cowboys, wagon wheels, lariats, and six shooters take center stage on this 1950s tablecloth. The set comes with four napkins. *Photo taken at West Bay Common School Children's Museum, League City, Texas.*
Measurements: 54x54 inches
Price Range: $225-$250

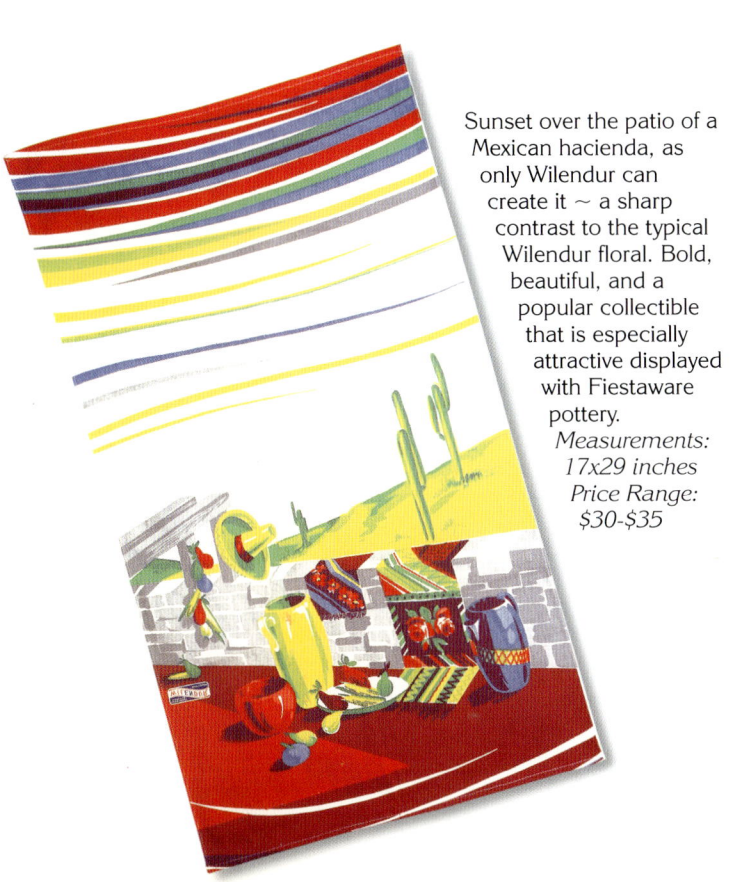

Sunset over the patio of a Mexican hacienda, as only Wilendur can create it ~ a sharp contrast to the typical Wilendur floral. Bold, beautiful, and a popular collectible that is especially attractive displayed with Fiestaware pottery.
Measurements: 17x29 inches
Price Range: $30-$35

A diminutive linen conversational towel from the maker Victory K&B featuring a pioneer lady and a Conestoga wagon being pulled by an ox. The Conestoga was developed in the mid-18th century by the Pennsylvania Dutch settlers of the Conestoga Valley in Lancaster, Pennsylvania. The distinctive shaped wagon was known as "the workhorse of the American road." No two of these custom built wagons were ever identical, but they shared the same distinct design, remarkable in its ability to prevent loads from shifting up and down hills. The Conestoga horses, one of the few breeds developed in the United States, were massive animals bred especially to haul these wagons around; teams of oxen were occasionally used as well. The single ox depicted on this towel would never have been able to handle a Conestoga alone. It is said the expression "I'll be there with bells on" originated with the Conestoga wagon. Its teams of horses often wore hoops of brass bells to warn others that the massive vehicle was approaching. Legend has it that if the Conestoga got stuck in the mud and required the assistance of any other wagoner, good manners would have them forfeit their bells to those who came to their rescue. Thus, arriving "with the bells on" was a source of pride to the drivers of these massive vehicles.
Measurements: 12x19 inches
Price Range: $20-$25

37

A very stubborn mule is being pulled by a bare-footed señor on this linen/cotton Mexican themed towel by Startex.
Measurements: 17x30 inches
Price Range: $25-$30

Full view of The Pride of Flanders Mexican towel below.

Boldly colored Pride of Flanders (Weil & Durrse, of Wilendur fame) Mexican themed towel featuring a donkey pulling a vegetable cart on pure, absorbent linen. The tablecloth in the background is the Wilendur Serape pattern, a look alike for a woven Mexican blanket. The colors used in the tablecloth are identical to the towel, and the pieces complement each other perfectly.
Measurements: 16x31 inches
Price Range: $30-$35

Colorful South of the Border themed Broderie Creations towel featuring a handsome young señor playing the guitar. The design is printed on only one end of this cotton towel. A cute chicken sits atop its perch and listens to the lovely music.
Measurements: 17x27 inches
Price Range: $35-$40

Nobody tops Broderie Creations for sheer whimsy and fun! Here, a delightful flamenco dancer is being chased by singing apples. This particular pair is linen, but the same pattern can also be found on heavy cotton. As with many towels by this manufacturer, the design is printed only on one end.
Measurements: 16x29 inches
Price Range: $35-$40 inches

Step up to the bar, pardner ~ in this western saloon you'll find mugs of beer for a nickel and an advertisement for an upcoming performance of "The Floradora Girls." The Floradora Girls show began in New York in 1900 and became one of the first successful Broadway musicals of the 20th century, running for 552 performances. The restoration of a young woman's stolen inheritance was the premise of this romantic musical based on a book by Owen Hall. The highlight of the show was its chorus line of six young women; each exactly 5 feet 4 inches tall and weighing 130 pounds. They captured many a heart and legend has it that they all married millionaires. Of note, the original spelling of the show was "Florodora," but it became commonly misspelled as time passed.
Measurements: 16x28 inches
Price Range: $55-$60

Close-up of cowboy bar towel.

39

Colorful Mexican themed hand printed towel from Fruit of the Loom in the pattern Monterey. This piece is often mistaken for a Wilendur because of its repeating-pattern design and heavy cotton sailcloth. The towel retains a price tag of .49 cents from the Globe Store of Luzerne, Pennsylvania.
Measurements: 17x34 inches
Price Range: $25-30

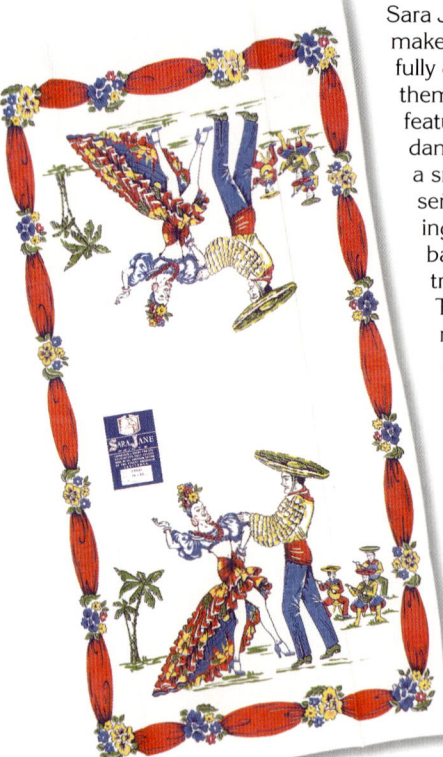

Sara Jane Prints is the maker of this beautifully detailed Mexican themed towel featuring a flamenco dancing señorita and a smartly attired señor accompanying her. In the background is a trio of guitarists. This towel is made of linen.
Measurements: 16x32 inches
Price Range: $20-25

Westward ho! A vibrant, colorful design of a covered wagon and pipe cactus by Startex. Cowboy-western themed textiles remain a steadily popular collectible and this one is a favorite.
Measurements: 15x29 inches
Price Range: $45-$50

A sandal-footed Mexican man wearing a ten-gallon sombrero carries a basket of vegetables. The tag reads "Superior Quality, Color Fast."
Measurements: 16x32 inches
Price Range: $20-$25

40

To Erin, this towel brings back memories of watching reruns of *The Cisco Kid* television show that aired from 1950-1956. Pancho was played by Leo Carrillo and was the Cisco Kid's faithful sidekick and comic foil. The show always ended with the two riding off into the sunset. The towel is a two-color hand printed design and the design is featured on one end of the towel only.
Measurements: 16x24 inches
Price Range: $20-$25

Wilendur Manjares tablecloth to match the towels below.

A trio of three Wilendur towels with Mexican pottery and gourds in fiesta colors. Wilendur did not specifically give names to their towels, but these were made to match their Manjares pattern tablecloth designed by John Madsen in March of 1940. This colorful design could also be found in green in addition to the colors shown here. *Photo taken at Quakertown Quilts, Friendswood, Texas.*
Measurements: 17x28 inches
Price Range: $30-$35

You have to look carefully at this Black Americana hand printed towel to see the anthropomorphic teapots and dishes. The waiter is carrying a serving tray with a cute teapot in one hand and in his other he carries the menu. This piece is pure linen and features color hues of blue, jadeite green, red and black. As with many Broderie designs, the pattern is printed on one end of the towel only.
Measurements: 16x28 inches
Price Range: $45-$50

If ever there was a stereotypical and politically incorrect Black Americana towel, it would be this one, featuring barefoot young children eating watermelon in the field. The towel is from the maker G&W Textiles, and as with other towels by this maker, the color and details are superb. While some people are offended by the unflattering portrayal of Black Americans in vintage textiles and kitchenware, others consider it an important part of our history during a period of time that should never be forgotten, lest it be repeated. No offense is meant in publishing the collection of Black Americana towels shown on the next few pages ~ they simply represent a part of our past portrayed in textile form, and as collectibles they are highly sought after by many.
Measurements: 15x28 inches
Price Range: $55-$75

Dinner time! The use of color is wonderful on this paper tagged towel by the maker Orlana. This extraordinarily detailed conversational design features a Mammy preparing the meal with the stereotypical kerchief tied to her head. The towel is hand printed on heavy weight cotton, and the tag reads "guaranteed colorfast."
Measurements: 16x27 inches
Price Range: $65-$75

42

Whimsical Black Americana towel depicting a woman knitting a sock while a young boy is snatching a bowl of fruit from the window above. This hand printed towel features color hues of red, green, blue, and black on a creamy linen.
Measurements: 16x28 inches
Price Range: $55-$60

A bright plaid border surrounding a man strumming the banjo and singing. It is no coincidence that black Americans are often portrayed carrying banjos ~ slaves from West Africa are originally thought to have brought that instrument to America. Notice the cotton boles on each side of the man. This towel is from the maker JS&S (Joseph Sultan and Sons) and a matching tablecloth was also available. It still retains the original .59 cent price tag from the J.N. Adam & Co. and came in a variety of colors.
Measurements: 17x27 inches
Price Range: $70-$75

Black chefs juggling kitchen implements, glasses, and pots and pans in the kitchen. A delightful cherry red and creamy towel of good quality linen.
Measurements: 16x30 inches
Price Range: $35-$40

A terrific pair of towels combining two very popular Broderie Creations themes, Black Americana and teapots. The smiling young fella is polishing the spout of his ribbon festooned teapot while the cheerful young lass is polishing the handle of her flower-embellished pot. Both these cotton towels are unused and retain remnants of their paper tags. Design is featured on one end of the towel(s) only.
Measurements: 16x28 inches
Price Range: $70-$75 each

An early Black American towel by Broderie Creations in deep, rich hues of three color printing.
Measurements: 17x27 inches
Price Range: $70-$75

43

Bold and very vivid colors are featured on this fantastic Black Americana hand printed towel featuring a Mammy carrying a tea tray. The towel is printed on smooth finished cotton and the design is printed on one end only.
Measurements: 16x28 inches
Price Range: $45-$50

A set of two darling Broderie Creations His & Hers towels. The first features a cook standing under a banner that reads "Baby Needs New Shoes" as he spills dice from his frying pan. The second towel of this series has a picture of Mammy's precious child on the wall with a banner reading "Mammy's lil' baby loves shortnin' bread." Design is printed on one end of the towels only.
Measurements: 17x28 inches
Price Range: $110-$125 set of two

A scarce whimsical Black Americana chef towel featuring a harried chef watching his pot bubbling over. The design is printed on one end of the towel only. This is a scarce pattern and rarely found in mint and unused condition.
Measurements: 17x26 inches
Price Range: $45-$50

44

*To Market to Market to Buy A Fat Pig…
Home again, home again, jiggety-jig;
To market, to market, to buy a fat hog;
Home again, home again, jiggety-jog.*

Designed by Ann Orr, this wonderful whimsical towel came in several different colors including yellow/brown, cornflower blue/navy, and jadeite/green. It has cross-over appeal to a variety of collectors ~ vintage textile connoisseurs, Black Americana collectors, and quilters. Ann Orr was best known as a 1930s quilt designer whose patterns have continually grown in both popularity and collectibility over the past seventy-five years. The original Martex Dry-Me-Dry paper tag is still affixed and is almost as charming as the towel itself.
Measurements: 17x34 inches
Price Range: $50-$55

A sweetly smiling mammy is drying dishes with soap bubbles floating all over the towel. The colors are deliberately soft and muted, not faded.
Measurements: 16x27 inches
Price Range: $45-$50

Close-up of the Martex Dry-Me-Dry paper tag, worthy of enjoyment on its own. The whimsical graphics depict a man with a pipe dangling from his lips, wearing a woman's ruffled apron while drying the dishes, and the slogan "Even a man can do a good job with a Martex Dry-Me-Dry." On March 26, 1936, Charles P. Coulter, Jr. as assignor to Wellington Sears, Co. (not to be confused with Sears-Roebuck department stores), applied for a patent on a special weave of spun rayon, linen, and cotton. Linen provided greater absorbency, cotton offered long wear, and adding a bit of rayon to the mix increased the speed at which the water evaporated, thus decreasing dish-drying time. The method of weave provided superior absorbency to other forms of crash fabrics produced in the past. This fabric was used extensively by Martex and marketed as the new wonder-fabric, "Dry-Me-Dry." The name Dry-Me-Dry was patented on June 28, 1938 and is U.S. Patent 2,122,175.

Here is a cartoonish mammy with her hair tied in a kerchief, singing a merry tune. The towel came in linen as well as a cotton/rayon blend and in a variety of color combinations. The "mammy" image grew in popularity from the late 1870s through the late 1960s, in large part due to the advertising industry. The image of mammy, often comically portrayed, was considered a wholesome and trusted pitchperson and was used to sell almost every household item ~ breakfast foods, soaps and detergents, beverages, baking supplies, and even ash trays. The best known and most successful use of mammy's image in advertising was (and still is) Aunt Jemima®, although her image has changed dramatically over the century. What was once a plump, comical, kerchief-clad figure has slimmed down into a lovely, modern woman.
Measurements: 16x27 inches
Price Range: $45-55

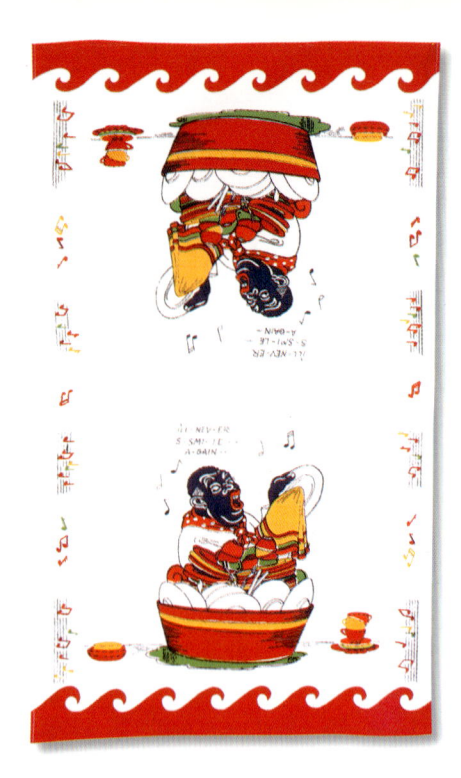

This older black man is up to his elbows in dishes, crooning a song first sung by Tommy Dorsey and made famous by Frank Sinatra ~ "I'll Never Smile Again." The song was written in 1939 by Canadian Ruth Lowe following the death of her husband after only a brief one-year marriage. The melancholy lyrics to the song go as follows:

I'll never smile again
Until I smile at you
I'll never laugh again
What good would it do
For tears would fill my eyes
My heart would realize
That our romance is true
I'll never love again
I'm so in love with you
I'll never thrill again
To somebody new
Within my heart
I know I will never start
To smile again
Until I smile at you
Within my heart
I know I will never start
To smile again
Until I smile at you.

The towel is cotton with the design printed on both ends and retains its .29 cent price tag from MacDougall's. As with many vintage Black Americana textiles, this piece is currently being reproduced ~ use caution and buy from only reputable dealers to insure getting the real vintage item. This piece was printed as both a towel and a tablecloth.
Measurements: 16x27 inches
Price Range: $75-100

Left:
Cute Black Americana towel featuring a daddy and his daughter ~ she is reaching for his piece of watermelon. This towel is from the maker JS&S (Joseph Sultan and Sons) and also came as a tablecloth that is so highly collectible it is being reproduced. There is no doubt this one is the original, as it still retains its .69 cent price tag from J.N. Adam & Company of Buffalo, New York. The store was in business until 1959. The hand made doll that is pictured with this towel is from the collection of Erin Henderson and is circa 1954.
Measurements: 16x27 inches
Price Range: $70-$75

Chapter 4
Happy Couples and Funny Faces

Happy people and funny faces were an endearing theme on many vintage towels, bringing humor and wit to otherwise tedious kitchen chores. These scenic towels were parodies of real life with all of its ups, downs, and comedic pitfalls. Occasionally, the expressions on the subjects of the towels are sour or laughably ludicrous, which just makes us grin even more!

Full view of bride and groom towel.

Get me to the church on time! A dapper groom and his prim bride pose for their wedding photo ~ towels such as this made lovely wedding shower gifts. It is made of absorbent linen and is quite generously sized, though somewhat faded, and the lower value reflects that imperfection. If perfect and unused, the value would double.
Measurements: 21x31 inches
Price Range: $15-$20

Two doves are putting the finishing touches on a wedding cake already laden with pink roses and putti. A jet black background adds a dramatic touch to this Martex Dry-Me-Dry towel. This uncommon wedding cake pattern was found with its original paper tag and washing instructions affixed to the back side. See page 45 for more information about the Dry-Me-Dry patent.
Measurements: 20x30 inches
Price Range: $45-$50

The first in a series of "Life Can Be Beautiful" towels by P&S Creations (nicknamed for the newspaper headline the man is reading) ~ some of Yvonne's very favorites. The comical series depicts life before and after marriage and children. They came in both linen and heavy cotton, which accounts for some of the color variation you see in the next two photos.
Measurements: 16x28 inches
Price Range: $40-$50 each

Apparently, everything prior to children is rosy and romantic. But things soon change…

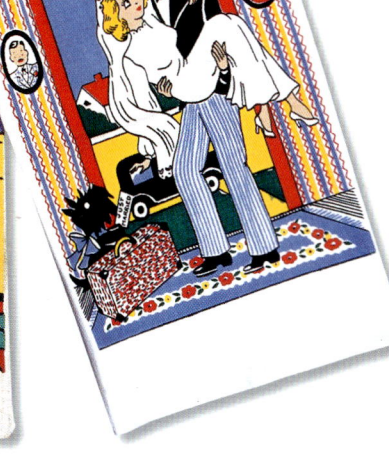

…with the arrival of baby number one, followed in rapid succession by babies number two and three. It looks like Papa is stuck with the lion's share of the childrearing and housework ~ is it like that in *your* house???

Blissful newlyweds drying the dishes ~ given the comical nature of so many of these vintage towels, we can't help but wonder what it will be like when the honeymoon is over!
Measurements: 15x29 inches
Price Range: $30-35

Close-up of blissful newlyweds towel.

50

The sampler in the background of this towel reads "Home is What We Make It" and obviously *this* home is a happy one. Pop is jumping up and down while Junior is trying to lasso him, and the baby on Mom's lap is delighted by the whole scene. Another P&S Creation by the makers of "Perma-Kleen" tablecloths.
Measurements: 17x28 inches
Price Range: $30-$35

A fair division of labor? The woman of the house is up to her elbows in dish suds while the husband takes forty winks in the backyard hammock. Next, looking rather befuddled, hubby attempts to cook while the wife reads the latest issue of a fashion magazine. Both towels are unused and made of cotton.
Measurements: 17x27 inches
Price Range: $30-$35 each

"You'll look sweet upon the seat of a bicycle built for two." A darling Gay '90s themed towel by Artmart Decropak with colorful graphics on heavy cotton.
Measurements: 16x26 inches
Price Range: $35-45

A very disgruntled looking husband glares at the flat tire on his "horseless carriage" while his lovely wife smiles happily ~ she obviously has complete confidence in his ability to fix it and still get them to the picnic on time. Automobiles were first developed in the late 1800s. These horseless carriages were expensive, slow, and broke down often. The roads they traveled were largely comprised of unpaved wagon tracks, which caused many flat tires and frustrated drivers! This whimsical design is printed on one end of the cotton towel only.
Measurements: 17x26 inches
Price Range: $25-$30

A darling duo of towels by Paragon featuring young children in cheerful ethnic dress. They retain their original Paragon "hand colored, boil proof" tag as well as the .59 cent price tag from Bowman and Company.
Measurements: 17x29 inches
Price Range: $25-$30 each

Two wonderful novelty towels by Overtex on natural linen. Their tag boasts "quality products" and is written across a world logo with a 1940s era airplane flying overhead and a ship in the water underneath. It appears this couple has fairly divided up the housework, though hubby looks none too thrilled at the prospect of having to do dishes *and* watch the baby. Both towels feature the design printed on one end only. The towel with the woman can be found in the 1943 Montgomery Wards catalog for 52 cents.
Measurements: 17x25 inches
Price Range: $75-$80 set

53

Three whimsical Gay '90s themed towels with amusing (if *very* slightly risqué) graphics ~ they are not only Yvonne's favorite series, but a favorite among many other collectors as well.
Measurements: 17x27 inches
Price Range: $40-$45 each

"With a Wink and a Smile" ~ Gramps is shaking the cocktails and Granny is holding the glasses…it must be martini time. A pair of wonderful whimsical linen towels edged along the bottom with a polka dot border of ruffled red chintz. The paper tag reads Progress Imported Pure Linen, T.S. & G., Inc. ~ the initials stand for the manufacturer Tobin, Sporn, and Glaser.
Measurements: 17x 25 inches
Price Range: $60-$75 set

Get your red hot dogs here! A whimsical farmer's market towel by All Time Towels-Original Creations. Hubby looks a tad upset ~ could it be he's miffed at the vendor who is making eyes at his lovely wife? This cotton towel still retains its original .49 cent price sticker from J.C. Penney Co. The design is printed on one end of the towel only.
Measurements: 18x27 inches
Price Range: $25-$30

54

A darling duo of musical towels with lyrics from some old classic songs ~ "In My Merry Oldsmobile" and "Dear Old Girl." "In My Merry Oldsmobile" (1905) is believed to be the first automobile song ever written, inspired by the successful completion of the first transcontinental race across questionable and bumpy roads from New York City to Portland, Oregon in just forty-four days.

Chorus: Come away with me Lucile in my merry Oldsmobile
Down the road of life we'll fly automo-bubbling you and I.
To the church we'll swiftly steal, then our wedding bells will peal,
You can go as far as you like with me, In my merry Oldsmobile.

These towels still have their 4/.94 cent price tags from the *original* Boston Store in Chicago. This icon of Victorian era marketing and merchandising closed its doors in July of 1948.
Measurements: 17x29 inches
Price Range: $30-$35 each

"When Irish Eyes are Smiling" ~ a border of shamrocks and leprechauns surrounds an attractive dancing couple. This seasonal favorite often commands a higher price when bought or sold near St. Patrick's Day.
Measurements 16x26 inches
Price Range: $30-$35

Darling graphics on this towel! On one end, Papa is playing the bagpipes while his lad and lassie dance ~ on the other side, he rests with his Scottie dog while Mother serves tea. A border of Scottish thistle completes the picture perfectly.
Measurements: 16x28 inches
Price Range: $35-$40

Ahhhh…young love! This towel by JBM still retains its original .49 cent price tag from J.C. Penney Co.
Measurements: 17x27 inches
Price Range: $25-$30

A duo of Broderie towels in mixed fabrics. The cheery kitchen lady print is made from linen and the happy farmer is a cotton/linen blend. As is so often found with Broderie Creations towels, the design is on one end only. *Photo taken at Butler's Courtyard, League City, Texas.*
Measurements: 16x29 inches
Price Range: $40-$45 each

Broderie lady with horse.
Measurements: 16x29 inches
Price Range: $40-$45

The singing teapot appears to have startled this Broderie lady.
Measurements: 17x27 inches
Price Range: $40-$45

It appears we are peeking in through a window at two busy friends washing and drying dishes ~ perhaps they have just finished their afternoon tea? This particular towel also came as a tablecloth and is a highly sought after collectible. A charming conversational, it still retains its original Broderie Creations paper tag stating that it is lintless and absorbent. The design is printed on one end of the towel only.
Measurements: 16x28 inches
Price Range: $55-$60

Two darling Broderie towels ~ a baker carrying a cake and a cook reaching for her cook book. Both are pure linen with the design on one end only.
Measurements: 16x28 inches
Price Range: $40-$45

Broderie happy farmer in garden and tea lady on pure linen. The farmer is similar to the design on page 56 but with several notable variations.
Measurements: 16x27 inches
Price Range: $40-$45

Broderie teapot girl ~ a highly popular design with collectors. They say imitation is the most sincere form of flattery...a very similar design was also made by Bucilla. Which came first is only a matter of speculation, but a great many Broderie and Bucilla look-alike patterns fool even the most seasoned collectors. Sara Jane Prints also produced a line of towels with graphics similar to Broderie.
Measurements: 16x28 inches
Price Range: $40-$45

57

One of Erin's favorite pair of Broderie Creations towels. One features a maid with the words "Good Morning" printed across her apron and carrying a tray with sugar and creamer, while the other features a maid with the words "Good Night" across her apron and carrying a tray with a candle, teapot, and apple. Both towels are mint with their paper tags still affixed and both are hand printed on pure linen.
Measurements: 16x29 inches
Price Range: $60-$65 each

Nobody poured on the charm the way Broderie did! This sweet whimsical towel features a cherry-cheeked granny surrounded by smiling anthropomorphic fruit as she knits. Check out the darling apple diving off the shelf…watch out below!
Measurements: 17x29 inches
Price Range: $40-$45

Perhaps room service did not see the "do not disturb" sign hanging on the door handle, because he's bringing up a steaming pot of tea and a wine list! This darling Broderie Creations towel is unused and still retains its original .39 cent price sticker from Vandever's on its back side. The design is printed on one end of the towel only.
Measurements: 16x29 inches
Price Range: $40-$45

Queen of the road ~ another wonderful towel from Broderie Creations featuring a hobo girl without a care in the world. A matching towel with a male hobo was also produced. The harvest colors of orange, jadeite green, yellow, and black make this a perfect fall decorating piece. This mint and unused towel is a scarce find that is seldom seen in the marketplace. It also came in burgundy on a creamy background.
Measurements: 15x29 inches
Price Range: $70-$75

It's raining posies! This darling Broderie Creations hand printed linen towel features a smiling young lady with a polka dot umbrella. In her arm she carries a basket full of eggs, some of which are hatching fuzzy little yellow chicks. This all cotton towel came in a variety of colors in both linen and a cotton/linen combo. Design is printed on one end of the towel only.
Measurements: 17x26 inches
Price Range: $35-$40

May we help you? A sweet chubby-cheeked waiter and maid duo by Broderie Creations. The fabric is pure linen and is hand printed in lovely fall colors of orange, yellow, jadeite green and black. Another scarce pattern that it not often found in the marketplace, especially in mint, unused condition.
Measurements: 16x29 inches
Price Range: $70-75

Broderie pig herder towel with the original .39 cent price tag from Vandever's. The tag has what appears to *possibly* be an inventory date-code from June of 1958.
Measurements 16x29 inches
Price Range: $40-$45

Cute conversational towels featuring Chinese chefs (or are they French?) preparing a culinary masterpiece while a little dog waits under the table for scraps to drop his way. These towels are pure linen and came in a variety of different combinations.
Measurements: 16x30 inches
Price Range: $35-$40

59

This bright, vivid towel was designed by Rosalie Forester and appears to be inspired by the Royal Doulton figurine, "Patchwork Quilt." Forester applied for a design patent for this towel on September 29, 1949 and was granted a seven year patent on February 7, 1950. A realistic and lifelike design and bold use of color by GW Prismacolor. The RN #14888 on the paper tag helped us identify "GW" as Grossman & Weissman, Inc., an importer, wholesaler, and manufacturer in New York.
Measurements: 16x27 inches
Price Range: $60-$65

A duo of towels inspired by the Royal Doulton figurines, "Balloon Man" and "Old Balloon Seller." The towels were designed by Rosalie Forester and produced in lifelike realism by GW Prismacolor. The Doulton experts we spoke with found no references in the Royal Doulton archive about textile design, so it is unknown whether these towels were produced with the company's blessing. Recently, Royal Doulton has licensed some of their designs for a variety of other home decorating items, but the figurine experts we questioned did not believe that was the case in the past. The towels can be found in the 1949 Sears, Roebuck and Co. catalog for only .55 cents each or 2/$1.05. *Photo taken at Butler's Courtyard, League City, Texas.*
Measurements: 16x27 inches
Price Range: $60-$65

Needlepoint canvas by Paragon, also inspired by the Royal Doulton "Old Balloon Seller."

Close-up of needlepoint "Balloon Man."

Royal Doulton advertisement featuring the "Balloon Man" figurine, from *Better Homes and Gardens Magazine*, May 1951.

61

It appears that this maid has thoughts of cocktails on her mind rather than doing the dishes, and she has convinced the unhappy child of the house to do the work for her. This pattern came in a variety of colors including red, green, blue, and yellow.
Measurements: 14x27 inches
Price Range: $20-25

Now did it say two tablespoons or two *teaspoons*? This befuddled housewife seems to be at a standstill in making her cherry pie with a cookbook in one hand, rolling pin in the other, and a priceless expression on her face. This cute kitchen scene towel by Leacock is made from pure linen and came in blue, green, red, and yellow. Do try the recipe and let us know how it tastes!
Measurements: 16x27 inches
Price Range: $25-$30

Cute conversational towel featuring a young woman with her groceries in hand and her little Scottie dog jumping up to greet her. The design is printed on one end of the towel only. This hand printed cotton towel is a P&S Creation by the makers of Perma Kleen tablecloths.
Measurements: 16x28 inches
Price Range: $35-45

A wonderful whimsical kitchen-themed towel with its Superior Quality tag still affixed. The towel features a woman dressed in early 1900s attire tending to her supper on a massive coal burning stove. A cute border detail features hurricane lamps, coal buckets, irons, kittens, rocking chairs, and potted plants. The paper tag on this unused cotton towel states that it is "color fast." According to the Callaway Textile Dictionary, color fast indicates that the colors are of sufficient fastness, particularly to light and washing, and that no noticeable change in color will take place during the normal life of the material. However, no fabric is *absolutely* colorfast, and care should still be used when washing these vintage beauties.
Measurements: 16x30 inches
Price Range: $25-$30

We don't know if it is the silly grins on the pixie-like faces, or the little bug atop the cake carrying off a cherry, but this hand printed Hadson towel brings a smile to our face! The towel is printed on light weight cotton.
Measurements: 14x28 inches
Price Range: $20-30

Charming pixie-like child on this crisp cotton towel from the Japanese maker, Hadson. To us, the design details are reminiscent of later Japanese animated cartoons. The design features the child eating an apple on one end of the towel; on the other end, he is climbing up a large grapevine while an owl looks on. This towel came in a variety of color combinations.
Measurements: 15x28 inches
Price Range: $20-25

A duo of "Keystone Cops" themed towels. The one on the right is signed by designer Tom Lamb, has a .59 cent price tag still affixed to it from Bowman & Co., and is made of linen. The one on the left is by Paragon and brags that it is "boil proof." Simply because of the Tom Lamb signature, the left-hand towel is about 20% more valuable than the other.
Measurements: 17x28 inches
Price Range: $30-$35

Looks like Pa didn't get his kitchen chores done ~ it is 10:00 p.m. and he's fast asleep in his chair with the dog and cat at his feet. Dishes, pots, and pans are stacked high in the sink. Bet he is going to catch it in the morning from his wife! A cute conversational linen towel from Society Creations. The design is featured on one end of towel only.
Measurements: 15x28 inches
Price Range: $25-$30

We think this butler needs to check his attitude at the door! This comical conversational towel features a rather snooty butler and a sweet house maid. The towel is made of heavy cotton sailcloth and is mint and unused.
Measurements: 15x29 inches
Price Range $25-$30

A charming Pennsylvania Dutch inspired pattern with a cameo of mother and daughter returning from the market. The lively border of bonnet clad girls and young boys is scattered with stylized tulips. The Penn-Dutch had a delightful obsession with the tulip motif, which appears abundantly in their art. Pottery, furniture, household linens, quilts, and even barn walls could all be found adorned in tulips. Their obsession with the colorful spring flower even inspired them to name a Pennsylvania stream after the bulb ~ Tulpehocken ~ which, according to one local source, means "banks heaped with tulips."
Measurements: 15x30 inches
Price Range: $25-$30

What was risqué by 1950s standards is a bit tamer today ~ we're quite sure this trio of towels by the Japanese company Imperial would've raised a few eyebrows in their day, both in the U.S. and in Japan, where they were manufactured. When the skirts of these gals are lifted, a view of wispy panties and a bare bottom can be seen.
Measurements: 15x27 inches
Price Range: $20-$25 each

64

Another slightly off-color set by Imperial that raises the age old question: "What is worn underneath the kilt?" According to Scottish custom and military regulation, no undergarments are to be worn, but there are exceptions to every rule. During Highland step dancing and athletic events, wearing undergarments is mandated to avoid embarrassing exposure. So the answer given by all good Scotsmen to the question of "what is worn beneath the kilt" is: "*Nothing* is worn ~ it is all in *first-class working order!* "
Measurements: 15x25 inches
Price Range: $45-$50 set

Whimsical scarecrow towel of pure, absorbent linen. Fall-themed towels, especially those with whimsical graphics, are a popular collectible and this one is no exception.
Photo taken at Butler's Courtyard, League City, Texas.
Measurements: 16x29 inches
Price Range: $45-$50

A comical butler and stern maid adorn this machine appliquéd tea towel set by Lady Christina Household Linens. Although this pair is not marked as such, we have found other items by this manufacturer marked "Made in Montreal by Decorative Linens Manufacturing."
Measurements: 17x25 inches
Price Range: $60-$65 set

65

A pinch of this, a dash of that…it looks like Mom's making fruit pie! A cute cotton conversational towel featuring a border of apples, pears, and cherries. This towel came in a variety of colors including red, green, burgundy, yellow, and blue.
Measurements: 16x26 inches
Price Range: $25-$30

There's so much going on with this linen towel we hardly know where to look first! What's up with the toucan in the tree?
Measurements: 15x29 inches
Price Range: $25-$30

Frolicking lambs surround a milkmaid and bovine center on this one-color beauty by Quality Prints (Leacock). The fabric content is a patented blend of 50% cotton and 50% linen called Dri-N-Dure. This towel is found in the 1943 Montgomery Ward catalog for .45 cents each or 2/.88 cents.
Measurements: 17x29 inches
Price Range: $20-$25

This colorful whimsical towel from Bucilla features a happy-go-lucky farmer scrambling around his barnyard chasing chickens. He appears to be thoroughly enjoying the romp! A similar pattern with the farmer's wife was also produced, as was a matching tablecloth. All are extremely collectible.
Measurements: 15x28 inches
Price Range: $25-$30

A "Spring Maid" towel by Springmaid, featuring the lovely lassie from the company logo on a carnation pink background. Vintage Springmaid towels are not readily found in the marketplace and this one is a real treat.
Measurements: 17x37 inches
Price Range: $50-$55

A fantastic piece of Springmaid history, this vintage card-table-sized tablecloth is a *game board* produced by Elliot White Springs as a tongue-in-cheek gift to business associates and friends. Dating from the New Deal period, circa 1936 to 1940, it expresses Colonel White's frustration with the government's policies and taxation of the manufacturing industry.

A different Springs mill is depicted in each corner of the cloth. The railroad running around the outside of the game is the Lancaster & Chester Railroad, which ran a 29 mile service line between the mills. (It is still operational today.) Colonel Springs had great fun with the idea of owning his own private railroad and made out train schedules, menus (in spite of the fact there was no dining car), and Vice Presidents. With his usual sense of whimsy (and somewhat risqué sense of humor), Springs designated burlesque stripper Gypsy Rose Lee as the train's "VP of Unveiling."

We haven't a clue how the game is actually played, but one must suspect it is similar to Parcheesi since the board is set up the same way. *From the collection of Michelle Hayes.*

Elliot White Springs wasn't the founder of Springs Mills, yet he can be single-handedly credited with the wildly successful growth of the company in a dark economic period when other textile mills were rapidly forced to shut their doors. His success, in large part, was due to his incredible sense of marketing and advertising. Many gorgeous women, known as Spring Maids, graced page after page of advertising for the company. While a bit tame by today's standards, the scantily clad women and somewhat bawdy ad text raised quite a few eyebrows ~ yet Springmaid textiles flew off the shelves as a result. These Springmaid calendars from 1951 and 1952 feature the talents of several artists of the day: Fritz Willis, James Montgomery Flagg, Arthur William Brown, Russell Patterson, and W. Turner. Shown in addition to the covers is the illustration for March 1951, by Fritz Willis. Also depicted in the calendars are some "in-house" staged photographs featuring "employees" that are very clever and funny as well. *Original image copyright Springs Industries, Inc. Used with permission.*

A pair of World War II themed towels from Broderie Creations. One features a dapper Army recruit drying a plate, the other a Navy seaman enjoying a "cup of joe." While the towels are not mint, their rarity makes them highly collectible. Over 400,000 men and women died serving in the armed forces during World War II, including Erin's uncle, Technical Sergeant Donald Hughes of Conrad, Iowa, who died of wounds received in combat in the South Pacific Theater. In May 2004, a memorial to honor those who served and gave their lives in World War II was finally completed. It is located across the reflecting pond from the Lincoln Memorial in Washington D.C.
Measurements: 17x26 inches
Price Range: $25-30 each, $60-$65 if mint

"Chicken Today, Feathers Tomorrow!" Ma and Pa Farmer dance a jig in anticipation of their Sunday dinner. This whimsical towel is based on the old philosophy that it's OK to eat chicken today, even if it means eating only feathers tomorrow ~ in other words, live for today! There are multiple design variations of this popular towel and it came in a variety of colors and fabric textures. Matching tablecloths were also produced. This one still has its original .39 cent price tag from W.T. Grant Company.
Measurements: 15x27 inches
Price Range: $30-$35

"Did you wind the clock," from the 1938 series by Calcot Hand Print featuring a portly man in a striped nightshirt. The fabric is pure linen with one color red printing ~ a delightful and scarce piece with its original paper tag attached.
Measurements: 17x32 inches
Price Range: $50-$55

Chapter 5
Cocktails Anyone?

Full view of Rey Aine cocktail towel.

A different scenic view represents each drink on this linen towel by Rey Aine ~ the "old fashioned" is depicted by a southern belle and her beau, a "side car" shows a picture of a vintage motorcycle and its side car, and of course the "Manhattan" beverage has a view of the New York skyline.
Measurements: 17x30 inches
Price Range: $45-$50

Gay 90s bar theme towel by P&S Creations, makers of Perma Kleen tablecloths. The sign reads "No Wolves Allowed" but that doesn't seem to deter the ungentlemanly behavior of *this* bar patron. Design on one end of the towel only.
Measurements: 16x28 inches
Price Range: $35-$40

This whimsically wonderful cocktail hour towel features an array of drinks that have come to life in anthropomorphic humanoid form. Multiple colors of this linen towel were produced by Leacock and matching cocktail napkins were also made.
Measurements: 16x26 inches
Price Range: $40-$45

If ever there were a reason to give up alcohol and cigarettes, the look on this woman's face would be motivation enough ~ she looks positively inebriated, smoking a cigarette, surrounded by cocktails and wisps of smoke. Three other hands appear out of nowhere, offering her another drink. The fabric of this head-spinning towel is lightweight cotton and it came in a variety of colors.
Measurements: 13x22 inches
Price Range: $45-$50

72

Absolutely adorable Gay 90s bar graphics on this duo of towels by Paragon Needlecraft Company.
Measurements: 16x28 inches
Price Range: $85-$90 set

Cocktails anyone? Drink recipes with the proper type of glass to use with each.
Measurements: 18x32 inches
Price Range: $25-$30

We're glad we were never invited to one of *his* cocktail parties! There are some questionable things behind the bar ~ hair oil, syrup of ipecac, turpentine, shellac, iodine, and ammonia. Apparently there is no such thing as a free lunch anymore either…the bar sign advertises a "free" lunch for only one dollar. This comical cocktail apron was manufactured by Barth and Dreyfuss.
Price Range: $25-$35

73

No whimsical vintage home bar could be complete without a comical apron for the bartender. Designed by Tony Sarg, this one features a trio of over-imbibed pink elephants singing "Sweet Adeline." A popular but difficult to find pattern that was also printed onto towels and tablecloths.
Price Range: $55-$60

This owl is dressed for a night on the towel, er…*town* as he sports a fancy top hat and tuxedo shirt. Swizzle sticks are scattered across the design, along with a book of matches and cigarettes burning in ash tray. A very 1950s color combination, hand printed on silky linen.
Measurements: 15x29 inches
Price Range: $30-$35

Most cocktail themed aprons were designed with the man of the house in mind.
Price Range: $25-$35

Step up to the bar and sink into an overstuffed stool ~ an assortment of cocktails await your selection! Choose from beer, martini, old fashioned, and brandy on this linen towel by Town and Country Linen Company of Lakewood, New Jersey.
Measurements 15x28 inches
Price Range: $20-25

74

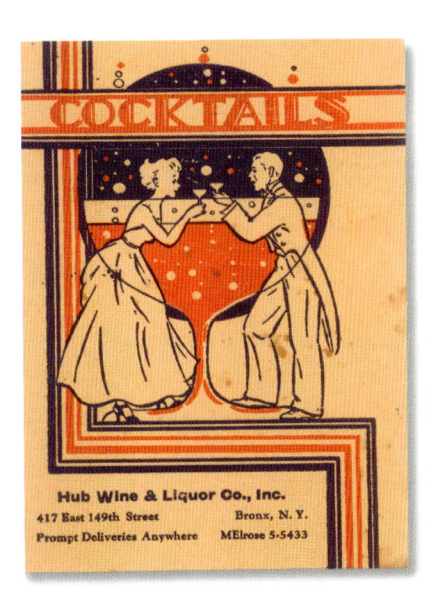

Two vintage cocktail books with instructions on how to mix your favorite drink. One is a giveaway from the Munson Steamship Line from a sail to Cuba, the other is from a New York liquor store that "offers its choice selection of wines and liquors to help you mix your cocktails properly so that you may enjoy them." We especially enjoy the poem written in one of these booklets: *"If on my theme I rightly think, there are five reasons why men drink, – Good wine, a friend, because I'm dry, Or lest I should be by and by, Or any other reason why."* ~ John Sirmond.

A cocktail collector's favorite ~ the "message in a bottle" themed towel featuring bottles floating in a fish-filled sea. The message stuffed inside reads "HELP…nearest bar on your right." You might assume that sending a message in a fragile glass bottle would never survive a rough ocean, but a well sealed bottle is a seaworthy object that can bob safely through rough seas that might otherwise sink a large ship. In the mid 1950s, divers off the coast of England recovered treasure from a ship that sunk 250 years previously, including eighteen liquor bottles. The alcohol inside was past the point of being drinkable, but the bottles themselves were perfect. This same pattern has also been found with a Lois Long signature, although this one is unsigned.
Measurements: 14x26 inches
Price Range: $25-$30

Bubblegum pink grapes and wine bottles against a cream linen background. This Belcrest Print towel has the same design on each end. *Photo taken at Butler's Courtyard, League City, Texas.*
Measurements: 17x29 inches
Price Range: $35-$40

75

Chapter 6
Sets and Stripes

Thrifty homemakers never wasted a scrap, as is obvious in this vintage Depression Era quilt. In addition to feed sack and period fabrics, vintage toweling was used to piece the bear paw pattern. *Photo taken at Quakertown Quilts, Friendswood, Texas.*

An assortment of very luxurious linen damask towels with a subtle teapot, sugar bowl, and creamer as the design elements down the center. Towels such as these would have been used for slightly dressier occasions where a vivid print design would not have been as appropriate.
Measurements: 21x29 inches
Price Range: $20-$25 each

If the following three sets of towels look similar to you, it's because they were all made for Barth & Dreyfuss of California and packaged under different labels ~ this boxed set sports the Terry Treasure label, a name that was first used by B&D in 1960.
Price Range: $75-$80

Another boxed set of six kitchen towels by Royal Terry of California, a Barth & Dreyfuss label that was first used by the company in 1952. The set depicts colonial women doing the traditional days of the week chores: Monday washing, Tuesday ironing, Wednesday sewing, Thursday cleaning, Friday shopping, and Saturday baking. These decorative ensembles were often given as housewarming and other celebratory gifts.
Price Range: $75-$80

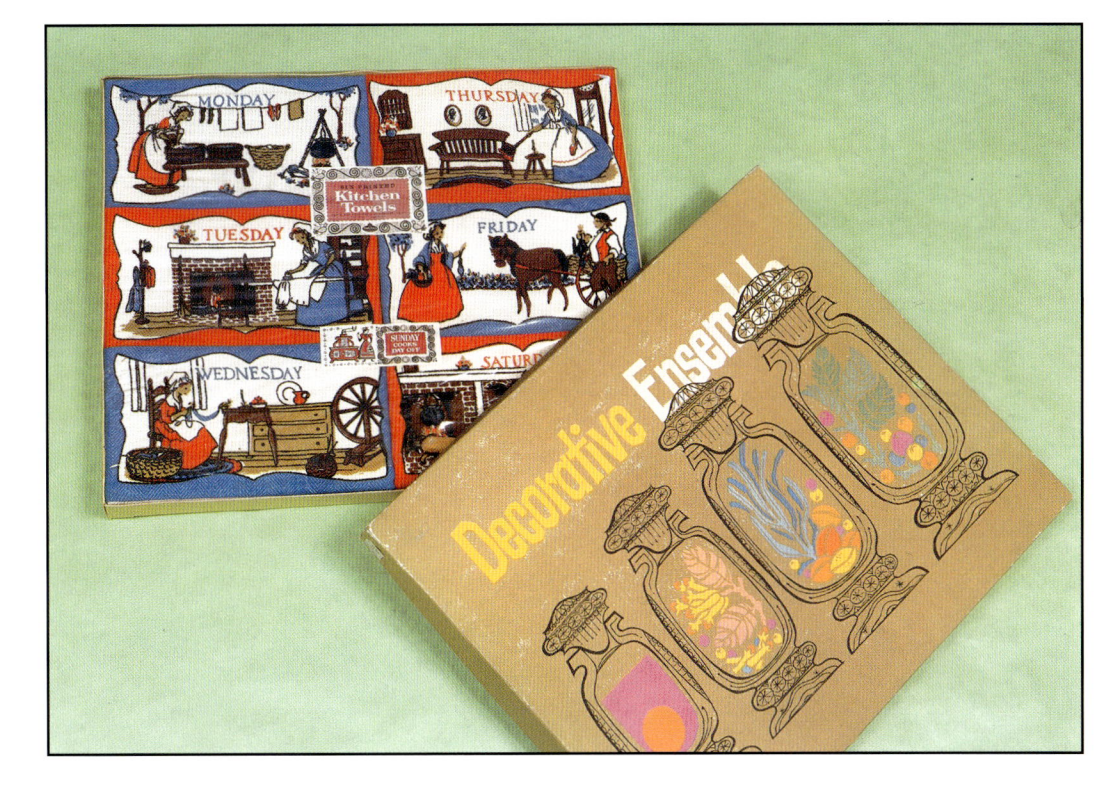

And yet another Royal Terry of California towel ensemble. Notice that the boxed sets generally include only six towels, with a note that "Sunday is the cook's day off." Since most housewives don't *get* a day off, we suspect the real reason is because only six would fit neatly in the box. Whatever the reason, we're sure housewives loved the notion!
Price Range: $75-$80

77

Carol Creation seven piece kitchen ensemble, consisting of two tea towels, one hostess apron, two pot holders, and a salad fork and spoon.
Price Range: $40-$45

Two boxed gift sets by Simtex Stevens. Coordinating kitchen ensembles were all the rage in the 1950s and 1960s ~ matching pieces were sold either by the set or individually and made terrific hostess gifts. Both of these sets consist of a terry hostess apron (that boasts it never needs ironing), hand printed sailcloth tablecloth of Wondercare Drip Dry, and a terry kitchen towel. Both sets are mint and have never been opened.
Price Range: $65-$70 per set

An assortment of striped and polka dotted towels ~ the workhorses of the kitchen, more utilitarian than good looking.
Price Range: $15-$20 each

Not all vintage toweling was designed for beauty alone ~ ordinary, utilitarian towels were absorbent, functional, and affordable. They were made from a variety of fabric blends. These mixed-weave textiles were often referred to as "crash linen," a coarse, plain weave fabric in various mixtures of linen, cotton, or rayon. The linen provided greater absorbency and the cotton offered long wear. Adding rayon increased the speed at which the water evaporated. These Morgan Jones and Cannon Rapidry towels were designed to be put to tough use in the kitchen. The packages of Morgan-Jones striped dish towels were woven with the "new 'moralin' yarn, a scientific blend of fibers made from cotton, rayon, and linen producing new high standards of durability and absorption and lasting quality."
Price Range: $15-$20 per towel

An assortment of striped linen towels in bright primary colors.
Price Range: $15-$20 each

Boxed set of four hand printed Color Craft towels featuring a day in the life of Dad ~ breakfast with the wife, lunch on the run, dinner with the family, and a late night snack with his faithful dog companion.
Measurements: 17x28 inches
Price Range: $50-$55

Vintage magazine advertisement for Morgan-Jones' dish cloths. "Lucky the bride-to-be ~ lucky *any* home-maker ~ who gets caught in a shower like this! Housewives from coast to coast praise Morgan-Jones' kitchen cottons for their soft absorbency and gay colorings. These fine quality cottons are so popular you'll find them in stores everywhere, singly or packaged. Look for the special cellophane and ever-so-welcome gift packages!"

Cannon gift set containing two towels with a Dutch motif. Coordinating tablecloths were also available in the same pattern.
Price Range: $25-$30

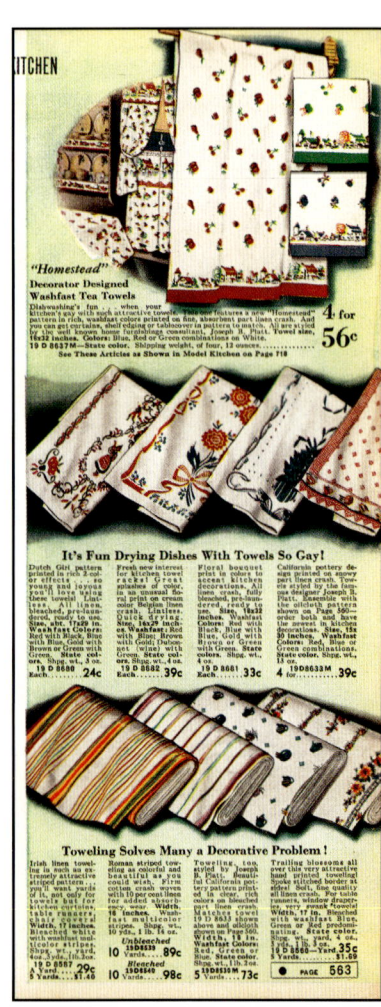

Sears Fall-Winter 1939-1940 catalog page with such tempting captions as "It's fun drying dishes with towels so gay!" and "Toweling solves many a decorative problem!"

Boxed set by Cannon consisting of a fringed apron, two kitchen towels, and one potholder. Gingham check provides the background for anthropomorphic veggies playing musical instruments. It doesn't seem to concern them that they may be on the menu!
Price Range: $25-$30

Small in stature, large in advertising bang ~ this boxed kitchen towel was a free bonus with a purchase of Lever Brothers detergent. The box reads: "Inside this box is a gift for you…New Style, Candy-Striped, Cannon Kitchen Towel!" Thrifty housewives could collect an entire set of towels at no cost.
Price Range: $10-$15

Below:
Historic Boott Mills of Lowell, Massachusetts is the maker of these four unused towels, each machine embroidered with the word "kitchen" in coordinating colors. The paper sticker affixed states these are "Dry Well" utility towels: "maximum absorbency, double thread, for kitchen and general use, and clean-ready for use." They are shown here with a Shawnee Granny Ann teapot of the same mid 1940s era. Boott Mills claims the distinction of being one of the oldest surviving mill complexes and today it is part of the Lowell National Historic Park. Be sure to see the manufacturer section in the back of this book for more Boott Mills history.
Measurements: 16x30 inches
Price Range: $50-$55 set of four

Many vintage kitchens were dressed in a multitude of matching decorating pieces ~ towels, toaster and mixer covers, oven mitts, doilies, aprons, tablecloths, napkins, curtains, and even decals for kitchen cabinets could be purchased in coordinating patterns. Perhaps homemakers of the day were unfamiliar with the expression "less is more," as often the effect could be a bit overpowering by modern standards. *This* vintage set by Bucilla would have been adorable when used in moderation. The pattern is called "Rose Petal" and each little blossom is a raised appliquéd patch, giving a three dimensional effect to the design.
Price Range: $75-$90

Set of six Gay 90s themed kitchen towels by Excello ~ design copyrighted 1948. The tag reads "Six towels that bring back the 'Good Old Days' in gay, color fast, hand blocked designs." The fabric is super-absorbent flour-sack-type cotton, a real workhorse in the kitchen.
Price Range: $75-$80

Here is proof that a utility towel need not be plain ~ fabulous fabric quality and understated design make this one special. Luxurious Irish linen with a touch of cotton thrown in, this towel by Gribbons has a French blue border of kitchen utensils and stemware. Gribbons first began production in 1923 and was best known for their quality fabrics (notably their linen and cotton damask) as well as embroidered linen. All towels we've seen to date with the Gribbons logo have been of exceptional quality. *From the collection of Sharon Stark of www.RickRack.com.*
Measurements: 18x30 inches
Price Range: $30-$35

"Hanson, The Symbol of Quality" ~ this great rooster-themed gift ensemble includes one printed dish cloth, one all purpose cloth, and one feather duster, all *very* cleverly packaged so that that duster is the rooster's tail.
Price Range: $45-60

This boxed set by Martex provides "charm for the kitchen in harmonizing ensembles." Another clever use of packaging, as the box is cut out in the shape of a teapot and two cups, allowing the buyer to see the towels within. Not only a nice collectible item for the kitchen textile connoisseur, but also for those who collect Black Americana…see label below. A rare find in mint and unused condition.
Price Range: $75-100

Close-up the Martex boxed set side panel, depicting a black mammy and child stirring a large cauldron. The contents of the kit are listed as: one Turkish towel [a.k.a. terry cloth], two utility cloths, two dish towels of cotton and linen, and two pot holders.

Chapter 7
Designers

Full view of C.P. Meier rabbit stew towel.

A simply darling rabbit stew towel signed by C.P. Meier and advising "First catch your rabbit"…but it appears he has no intention of being snared. *Photo taken at Butler's Courtyard, League City, Texas.*
Measurements: 15x28 inches
Price Range: $50-$55

A Virginia Zito design of asparagus, peas, veggies, linen, carrots, radishes, and green onions on natural linen.
Measurements: 16x29 inches
Price Range: $25-$30

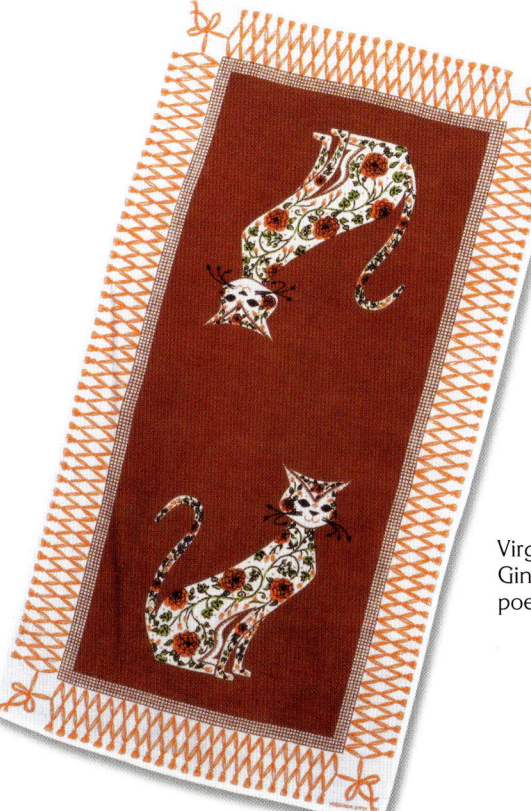

This "Morning Inspection" towel signed Zito shows the staff lined up and ready for work. While the signature would make it easy to mistake this for a *Virginia* Zito design, the artist was actually famed European caricaturist, Vinzento Zito. A remarkable talent, Zito was the youngest student to attend Académie des beaux-arts (Academy of Fine Arts) in France and later attend the Royal Beaux Art in Rome on scholarship. He excelled in every art medium and worked at lightning fast speed. Despite his talent, Zito found himself penniless on the streets of Paris and tried "zipping" out carticatures for resturant patrons to earn a meal. His talent quickly earned him fame and soon his skills were in demand the world over. Zito sketched kings and queens, wealthy businessmen, heads of State, famous actors and actresses, and even maharajah ~ and he did so as he *honestly* saw them; sometimes in a flattering portrayal, and sometimes without pity. He was particularly well-known for his delightful and often humorous sketches of dogs and published a collection of his canine sketches in *Dogs By Zito* in 1936. Another collection of his works, *Monkey Business,* was published in 1944. Zito's whimsical art work transfers well into textile design ~ while he was famous within cartooning and caricature circles, we find him quite an unrecognized talent in the textile world. In our opinion, his towels do not command a price for which they are worthy.
Measurements: 17x27 inches
Price Range: $25-$30

Virginia Zito designed this modernistic Calico Cat linen towel and a coordinating Gingham Dog towel as well. The Calico Cat and Gingham Dog were featured in a poem called "The Duel" by Eugene Field:

"…the gingham dog and the calico cat,
side by side on the table sat;
'twas half-past twelve, and (what do you think!)
Nor one nor t'other had slept a wink!
The old Dutch clock and the Chinese plate
Appeared to know as sure as fate
There was going to be a terrible spat."

Measurements: 15x28 inches
Price Range: $25-$30

85

Another Vinzento Zito design featuring the milkman and ice man at the service door being welcomed (or not??) by a shapely maid ~ with her hands on her hips, she looks a bit perturbed. Design is hand printed on one end of this natural linen towel.
Measurements: 15x27 inches
Price Range: $20-$25

"Something's Burning!" A great firefighter themed towel by designer Tammis Keefe. This linen towel can be found in a variety of colors, including gold, green, red, blue, and brown.
Measurements: 16x29 inches
Price Range: $30-$35

French dressing towel by Tammis Keefe. Keefe (born in California as Margaret Thomas Keefe in 1920) was a prolific textile artist who excelled in a multitude of different mediums. She was best known for her handkerchiefs (produced by Kimball from 1947 to 1958), but also designed scarves (for Kimball beginning in 1953), tablecloths, towels, cocktail napkins, home furnishing fabrics, clothing fabric for men, greeting cards, pottery, and even a "fortune telling" board game. It seems that just about everything Tammis touched is pure gold to collectors ~ her whimsical handkerchiefs command top dollar in the collectible marketplace, as do her towels and table linens. Cocktail napkins by Tammis Keefe are also a favorite of collectors. While she did produce some geometric and floral patterns, they do not hold the value of her whimsical pieces. Ms. Keefe passed away in 1960.
Measurements: 16x30 inches
Price Range: $40-$45

Whimsical animal designs by Tammis Keefe are some of her most popular collectible patterns. This mama cat is obviously quite proud of her little ones. Ms. Keefe's talent and sense of fun shine through with this pattern, which was also available in blue, aqua, and coral red.
Measurements: 16x30 inches
Price Range: $50-$55

"Home Sweet Home/My House is My Castle" towel designed and signed by Tammis Keefe. The towel features a decidedly 1950s color palette and is warranted all linen on the foil tag.
Measurements: 16x30 inches
Price Range: $45-$50

"Bless this House" towel by Peg Thomas, the pseudonym used by Tammis Keefe in some of her designs. Towels with the Thomas signature are equally charming, yet do not command the price of a signed Keefe. Perhaps once word gets out that they are one and the same person, the value will rise.
Measurements: 16x30 inches
Price Range: $30-$35

Tammis Keefe must have fancied cats, as they show up often in her work. These *adorable* towels are a favorite among collectors as much for their wonderful, earthy colors as for their comical design.
Measurements: 16x30 inches
Price Range: $50-$55

Full view of Tammis Keefe Christmas towel, a vivid collector's favorite that came in green as well.
Measurements: 16x30 inches
Price Range: $50-$55

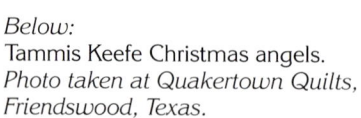

Below:
Tammis Keefe Christmas angels.
Photo taken at Quakertown Quilts, Friendswood, Texas.

Above:
Sailing ships, lobsters, cast iron pots, and the makings for clam chowder and baked beans bring Boston and New England to mind. This pure linen towel is designed and signed by Pat Pritchard. She also designed other towels in this "Americana Series" using a similar design layout and incorporating food items from other cities or regions such as New Orleans and the West. Little information is available about Ms. Pritchard. She was primarily a handkerchief designer for Kimball, although she produced towels, tablecloths, placemats, and dinnerware as well. All of the kitchen textiles we have seen with the Pritchard signature have been produced for Town House Decoratives. We know Pat Pritchard was actively designing throughout the 1950s and possibly into the early 1960s. Although quite nice, her towels do not command the prices of others with designer signatures.
Measurements: 16x28 inches
Price Range: $25-$30

Part of a series designed and signed by textile designer Pat Pritchard. This conversational towel has a decidedly New Orleans feel ~ bouillabaisse, shrimp Creole, fried chicken, banjos and trumpets, and the great paddle boats of the Mississippi. It is pure linen and still retains its sewn in label stating it is an Original from Town House Decoratives.
Measurements: 16x26 inches
Price Range: $25-$30

Another Pat Pritchard design, this one featuring items from the Wild West: trains, a frontier saloon, steak, spare ribs, and the Wells Fargo stage coach. The towel retains its original $1.00 price tag from the Boston Store and has been marked down to .50 cents.
Measurements: 16x26 inches
Price Range: $25-$30

Designer Luther Travis poses the age old question: "Which came first, the chicken or the egg?" Once overlooked by collectors as "not quite vintage enough," textiles with the Luther Travis signature have grown in both popularity and value in recent years. Travis studied to be an interior designer at Parson's School of Design, the New York School of Interior Design, and then the College of William and Mary, where he earned a B.A. in interior design and fine arts. He soon discovered that his interests lay more in textile design than interior decorating, so he returned to Parson's for a textile design certification. After only two short years in the job market, Travis was hired by Bloomcraft, where he designed a variety of textiles for the home, including linens for the kitchen, bed and bath, and wallpaper. His talent was well appreciated by the company and he was promoted up the corporate ladder to vice president of design. Travis described his thirty year tenure at Bloomcraft as "the most wonderful thing that ever happened in my life. It was work, but it didn't seem like it." While at Bloomcraft, he was active in freelance design as well, including such projects as greeting card design for upper-end department stores.

As evidenced in his primarily floral textile designs, Travis has a passion for plants and nature. In addition to a conservatory located at his Greenwich Village historical district home, he at one time had eight acres in New Jersey devoted to a collection of over 3,000 orchids. Since his retirement from textile design, Travis has entered prize orchids in shows across the country and has received a number of prestigious awards for his plants.
Measurements: 16x30 inches
Price Range: $25-$30

One of our favorite Luther Travis designs ~ a center row of colorful grapes bordered by black and white sketches of the same design. An oatmeal colored linen background adds just the right touch of elegance to this beautiful Fallani & Cohn towel.
Measurements: 17x30 inches
Price Range: $30-$35

Designer Victor Beals signed this charming conversational towel featuring the Longfellow House in Cambridge on one end and a New England harbor scene on the other. This hand printed cotton towel is from the maker Dutch Girl. Victor Beals was born on February 20, 1895 in Wuhu, China. How and when he came to America is sketchy, but we do know he studied art at the Vesper George School of Art, as well as under the tutelage of American painter Albert Henry Munsell (who is famous for developing a standardized color system). The majority of Beals' career was spent designing advertising art for travel companies (such as the Santa Fe Railroad) and vacation destinations (such as Puerto Rico), as well as creating cover art for major magazines. Beals also designed WWII war posters for the government, which are still widely collected. Textile designs by Victor Beals are a scarce find.
Measurements: 16x25 inches
Price Range: $45-$50

This striking towel was designed and signed by Mary Sarg (Mary Sarg Murphy, 1911-1986), daughter of famed illustrator, inventor, author, puppeteer, and textile designer Tony Sarg. "Don't Give Up the Ship" was the stirring battle cry shouted by an out-numbered Captain Oliver Perry during the Battle of Lake Erie in the War of 1812. Captain Perry went on to defeat the British and the motto "Don't Give Up the Ship" would became a national call to rally that is still used today.
Measurements: 16x28 inches
Price Range: $25-$30

Pull up your chair for a round of checkers in this country store themed linen towel by designer Lois Long for Town House Kitchen Decoratives. The towel is dated 1956 next to her signature. Long also designed towels for Kay Dee Hand Prints and Fallani & Cohn, with the majority of her designs dating from the 1950s to 1960s. In addition to textile design, Lois illustrated books, including *Mud Book*, written by her friend John Cage.
Measurements: 16x29 inches
Price Range: $20-$25

This darling cat towel was also designed by Mary Sarg. Born in London, England, Mary and her mother came to the United States in 1914 at the start of World War I. Father Tony Sarg soon joined them in Cincinnati, where they remained for a year before moving to New York. She studied her craft at the New York School of Applied Design For Women as well as the Art Students League in Phoenix. Mary began working under the tutelage of her famous father, decorating furniture, wallpaper, fabrics, children's clothing, and towels for the Tony Sarg Shops in New Hope and Nantucket. She quickly became a renowned artist in her own right whose portraits were sold in exclusive East Coast galleries. Today, a Mary Sarg Murphy painting commands a high price tag in the art world. Throughout the 1930s, Ms. Sarg also illustrated children's books and became well known for her artwork in such major magazines as *Today*, *Woman's Day*, and *Mademoiselle*. Beginning in 1923, Sarg summered with her family in Nantucket and became somewhat of a celebrity in the area. Two Nantucket newspapers ran a popular cartoon series created by Sarg, later compiled into one collection and published as the *Nantucket Blue Book*.

Very few textile designs can be found with the Mary Sarg signature. The original pure Belgian linen tag is still affixed, and a search of the Federal Trade Commission web site helped us identify the manufacturer as Edmond Dewan Company of New York (RN#18343).
Measurements: 16x29 inches
Price Range: $45-$50

"What's Cooking?" Part of a series of food-themed towels designed and signed by textile designer Lois Long. This towel features bratwurst grilling over an open campfire. The original Town House paper tag is still attached.
Measurements: 16x29 inches
Price Range: $25-$30

No book on vintage tea towels would be complete without at least *one* calendar towel! This 1964 Vera beauty is an exceptional example and one of the few we have seen signed by a popular designer. The concept of calendar towels began growing in popularity in the 1960s and peaked in the 1970s and 1980s. They were generally displayed, not used, so they are readily found in perfect condition. As a collectible, they are still extremely affordable and can found in the $5-$10 price range. Being a designer towel, this Vera would be slightly more pricey, yet still affordable.
Measurements: 16x28 inches
Price Range: $15-$20

Top right:
Vera used explosive color on this lemon-lime wine towel, vivid almost to the point of being blinding. Vera Neumann is one of the most famous women in the history of textile design and the first person known to sign her name to her textiles. For all of this, one would expect a wealth of information to be readily available about her, but that is not the case. Various sources of research have yielded contradictory pieces of information, but what we have included here appears to be accepted by most accounts. Vera Salaff Neumann (July 24, 1910 – June 18, 1993) studied at the prestigious Cooper Union College in the 1930s and later at The Traphagen School of Fashion Design. In either 1944 or 1946 (depending on the account), Vera, her husband George, and a friend named F. Werner Hamm began what would become the vast Vera empire. From the kitchen table of her New York City apartment, she screen printed her first order ~ silk placemats for the B. Altman department store. Altman's was so impressed that their following order was overwhelmingly large, and thus Vera's success began. Her bold, bright designs for scarves, apparel, furnishing fabrics, table linens, and towels were signed only with her first name. Vera once explained that it was only natural for her name to appear on her textiles, as each piece began as a signed painting before being printed onto cloth.

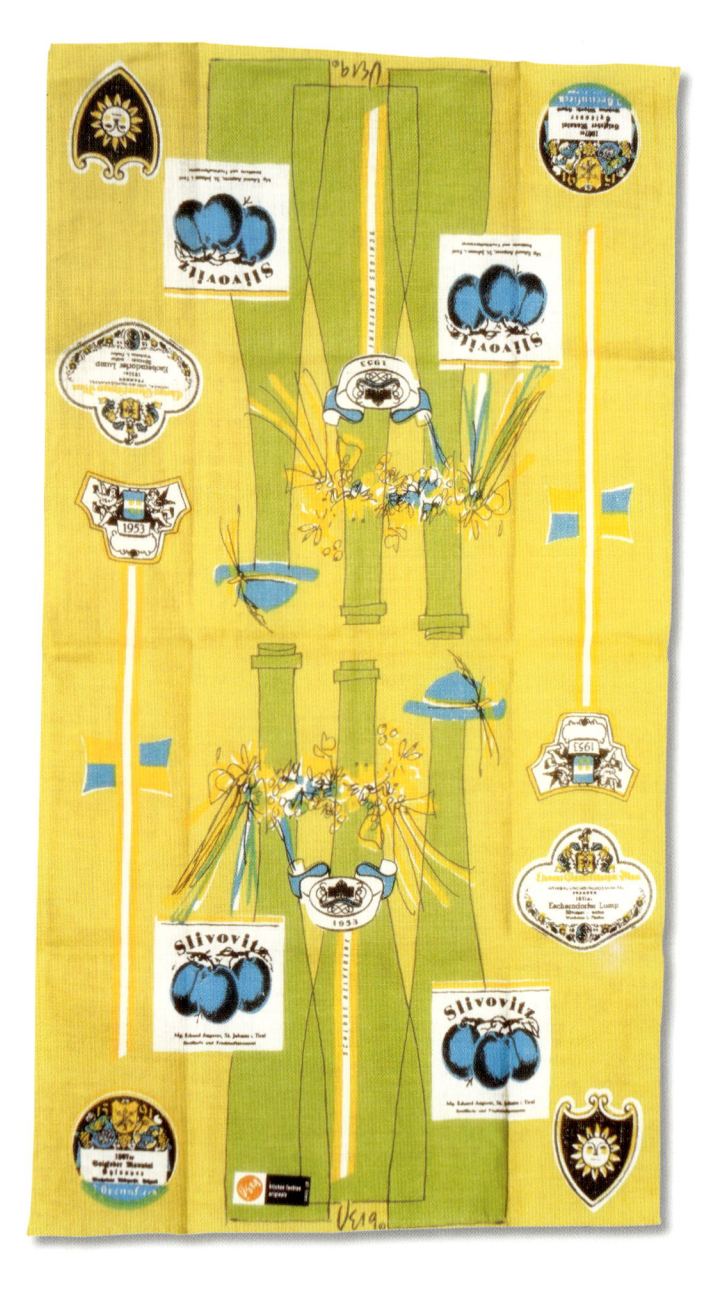

From approximately 1944/1946 until 1967, Vera was a freelance designer for F. Schumacher & Co. Earlier Vera designs feature a ladybug (a symbol of good luck) next to her signature. Some accounts say Vera signed the ladybug on her very first piece ~ others claim it began in the 1950s. The ladybug was used sporadically in her later creations, apparently only when the mood struck her. The inspiration for her bold, bright, stylized botanical art came from the Hudson River Valley where her studio and home were located. Vera enjoyed travel and picked up design ideas from around the world ~ the villas of Italy, museums in France, architecture in Spain, and modern Scandinavian sculpture all provided fuel for the talent and imagination of this brilliant designer. Of curious note, the dates of the wine bottle labels on this towel range from 1944 to 1967, which corresponds with the approximate dates of her free lance work for F. Schumacher and Co.
Measurements: 15x29
Price Range: $40-$45

Known for her abstract textile patterns and bold use of color, Vera once said that everything she designed began as a painting, as is well evidenced on these towels. Bold Monet-inspired splashes of color make up the poppies that cover the entire towel in an eye popping abstract design. The original paper tags are still affixed, declaring that the towels are made of pure Belgian linen. Vera textiles have experienced a steady rise in popularity in the past several years, with her towels rising in value much faster than her table linens. We can only speculate as to why this is the case ~ Yvonne, for example, has become enamored with Vera's towels because she finds the wild tablecloth designs to be overpowering on such a large scale, but absolute perfection on a smaller towel.
Measurements: 16x29 inches
Price Range: $40-$45

A set of three "Be An Angel" cherub towels signed by Richard Tucker (1903-1980). Richard Derby Tucker was born in New York City and began attending the Art Students League at the young age of sixteen. His career as an artist was temporarily placed on hold while he attended Harvard University, graduated, worked as an investment banker, and later commanded three Atlantic escort vessels during World War II. After returning home, he spent three more years at the Art Students League before finally realizing his dream of becoming a full time professional artist. From 1950 until his death, Tucker lived in Camden, Maine, where he spent long, diligent hours in his studio. Winters were generally spent in southern France and Portugal, perhaps gathering inspiration for his many works of art.

The monetary value of this trio of towels will vary depending on the purchaser ~ a towel collector might love them for their wonderfully fanciful cherub design, while a connoisseur of Richard Tucker's paintings will place a higher value on them for the rarity of having his art on a kitchen textile.
Measurements: 18x30 inches
Price Range: $50-$55 each

Festive Christmas towel signed by Edward C. Smith and dated 1953. Children's toys line the border and a toy train track circles the base of the Christmas tree. This charming towel is hand printed on cotton.
Measurements: 17x30 inches
Price Range: $30-$35

Right:
Edward C. Smith towel in its original Bestex Hand Prints packaging. The packaging and wording on the back side are identical to packaging we have found for the Kay Dee company:

"The Loveliest Kitchen Towel in All the Land!
This beautiful Bestex towel has been printed entirely by hand in guaranteed washable colors on the finest toweling fabric obtainable. These are the towels you have read about in the country's leading home furnishing magazines. They have been acclaimed as 'The Loveliest Kitchen Towels in All the Land'…so decorative they are conversation pieces as table-runners or chair backs; and have been cut and sewn into place-mats, curtains, and many similar colorful items. A beautiful, practical gift for a note of gaiety in any home.
Bestex Hand Prints, Hope Valley, Rhode Island."

Although the Kay Dee company representative knew of no connection between the two companies, we can't help but wonder at this curious coincidence. Please see page 121 for an example of the matching Kay Dee packaging.
Price Range: $30-$35

A matronly Pennsylvania Dutch hausfrau on baking day. On one end of the towel, Großmutter is rolling out pie dough. On the other end, she is removing a loaf of fresh bread from her outdoor Dutch oven. The two foods were not coincidentally depicted here. On baking day, earthenware pie plates (dubbed tulipware for their floral patterns) could be added to the Dutch oven and cooked at the same time as the bread without adding to the fuel cost. Pie was a favorite food of the Dutch, even to the point of being served at breakfast. This towel is signed by Edward C. Smith with a copyright date of 1952. Hidden in the ever-present Penn-Dutch border of tulips are the words "printed by hand." Written on the heavy kitchen crock is MAHL, the German word for meal.
Measurements: 16x30 inches
Price Range: $30-$35

94

Ripe red strawberries surround a vivid field of blossoms ~ this towel is signed "The Ryans" and was produced for Fallani & Cohn, Inc. Martin and Lorraine Ryan, a husband and wife team, were prolific designers of home fashions for the bed, bath, and kitchen with their art gracing dinnerware and a multitude of kitchen towels and tablecloths. Wallpaper, upholstery, and floor coverings also showcased the Ryans' signature flair for color and design, and their work was sought-after by many of the largest companies in the industry. Additionally, Lorraine's upholstery designs have had the distinction of being photographed on the cover of many major magazines.

Lorraine graduated with honors from the prestigious Parson's School of Design (notably, designer Luther Travis attended Parson's at the same time) and later attended the Art Students League of New York. After serving in the United States Army, Martin also attended the Art Students League, followed by studies at the Workshop School of Design. Martin wrote and published *The Ryan Report,* an often-quoted design forecast newsletter that helped shape the industry for ten years.

In 1968, this talented team occupied a studio off 39th street in New York City, where they employed two other artists. Martin and Lorraine saw an opening in the textile market that was not being adequately filled ~ a need for a completely coordinating, mix-and-match line of kitchen textiles. With this in mind, they designed, produced, and marketed their private "M&L Poppies" line to upscale retail stores such as Bloomingdale's. The product flew off the shelves and even eclipsed sales of Vera textiles for some time. This brought the dynamic designing duo to the attention of Fallani & Cohn. For the next eleven years (approximately 1969 to 1980, by Martin's recollection) they received annual contracts to design exclusively for the F&C brand. We found it interesting to learn that Martin & Lorraine were a true *team* in their designs ~ often one of the couple would start a design and pass it on to the other for completion!

Although retired from textile design, the couple still maintains an active and important place in the fine art community. Lorraine has received numerous awards for her exquisite work, which is exhibited across the country. Martin is accomplished in fine art as well, currently focusing his efforts on capturing the realism of wildlife scenes. He enjoys cartooning, and has posted some favorites on his web site (see the resource guide at the back of this book for a link).

Kitchen towels and tablecloths by "The Ryans" have enjoyed a rise in popularity among collectors in recent years as they pass from being "retro" into becoming truly "vintage." We believe the wise collector would be best served buying their designs now, while the prices are still reasonable.

Measurements: 16x28 inches
Price Range: $25-$30

Designed by Carrie Wilson, this linen towel features a recipe for crêpes suzette. Ms. Wilson designed this and numerous other kitchen linens for Edmond Dewan and Company of New York, and the "Styled by Dewan" logo usually appears somewhere in her designs. Many collectors have mistaken the signature for "Dervan" rather than Dewan…an error honestly made, as the cursive writing certainly isn't clear.
Measurements: 16x29 inches
Price Range: $15-20

95

Fresh doughnuts ~ a delightful Black Americana conversational towel by JBM signed by designer Tom Lamb (Thomas Babbitt Lamb, 1896-1988). Mammy is carrying a large bowl of freshly made doughnuts and the children are watching through the window. Lamb attended the Art Students League and New York University. His design career was diversified ~ Lamb was an accomplished cartoonist, illustrator, author of children's books, industrial designer, and inventor. Textile collectors know him best as a prolific designer of children's handkerchiefs, producing darling whimsical patterns that are highly collectible and bring top dollar. Towels, tablecloths, and napkins by this designer are a scarce treat.
Measurements: 16x25 inches
Price Range: $45-$50

A blinding orange, avocado green, red, and yellow rooster has earned this Georges Briard towel the affectionate nickname "the screaming chicken" ~ we can't help but love it for its retro funk. Jascha Brojdo was born in Russia to a wealthy Ukraine family. He migrated to Poland at the age of four and then to the United States in 1937. Brojdo enrolled in classes at the Art Institute of Chicago to study his craft. After serving in the American Army during World War II, he began his art career by hand painting blank trays. He was wise enough to realize that a name could make or break his success, and chose the pseudonym Georges Briard because he felt it lent his work an air of French sophistication. Over the next three decades, Briard became a household name associated with elegance and high style, designing a wide range of household items, barware, small household furnishings, linens, and tableware for such upper end department stores as Neiman Marcus. He was also careful not to leave middle class Americans out of his marketing plan, and designed several lines of moderately priced gift sets that were extremely popular wedding and hostess gifts. His textiles are not as common or as collectible as his other household items.
Measurements: 16x28
Price Range: $25-$30

Xavier Cugat (January 1, 1900 – October 27, 1990) was born Francisco de Asis Javier Cugat Mingall de Bru y Deulofeo in Gerona Spain. He immigrated to Cuba when he was five years old and then to the United States at the age of fifteen. Cugat was an accomplished violinist and was immediately hired to travel with the operatic tenor, Enrico Caruso. Although his music was well received by audiences around the world, Cugat was a perfectionist and wasn't pleased with his skills on the violin. He quit touring and began working as a caricaturist for the Los Angeles Times. The demanding deadlines didn't suit Cugat, so he quit and formed his own band, "Cugat and the Gigolos." Capturing the essence of the Cuban music of his childhood, he thoroughly captivated audiences with his intriguing tropical rhythm and melodies, which would later become known as the Rumba. For the next thirty years, he successfully navigated each turn in the music industry, changing the flavor of his records to fit the public's demands, and capitalizing on every dance trend from the cha-cha to the twist. Although the comic caricatures from his newspaper career were at one time in syndication, we have found only a few of his designs being captured on textiles; this is one of a scarce series. Even faded as this towel is, it is a rarity and commands a high price.
Measurements: 15x26 inches
Price Range: $60-$65

Ivan Bartlett signed linen towel featuring apple branches and butterflies. The original foil tag tells us it is hand printed by Leacock.
Measurements: 16x29 inches
Price Range: $25-$40

Shimmering golden roses sparkle against a turquoise background on this towel by designer Ivan Bartlett for Leacock. Mr. Bartlett was primarily known as a painter, illustrator, and lithographer and is listed in *Who Was Who in American Art*. He was born in Plainfield, Vermont in 1908 and studied at the renowned Chouinard School of Art in Los Angeles, California. Bartlett grew in fame through his work in Roosevelt's 1930s New Deal art projects, painting murals in California beach towns. One of his most famous murals is located in the stairway of Polytechnic High School in Long Beach, California, where Bartlett was an alumnus. In addition to being a muralist, he was a gifted painter of fine art, illustrator, engraver, and lithographer. During the 1940s to early 1950s, Bartlett worked as a textile and wallpaper designer as well, moving to New York City where his career flourished into the 1960s. He passed away in Andover, Massachusetts in 1976. Textile designs by Ivan Bartlett are harder to find than many designer names and command a consistently steady price. *Photo taken at Butler's Courtyard, League City Texas.*
Measurements: 16x28 inches
Price Range: $35-$40

The classic masterpiece of design, the Wilendur Royal Rose by Sergei Bogdanovich (1890-July 1970) and his wife Tamara (1905-1984). Although their work was unsigned, we consider the Bogdanovich duo to be among the most brilliant textile artists of the era and worthy of inclusion in this "designer" section. Throughout the 1930s to 1960s, floral motifs were by far the most popular designs printed on vintage towels and tablecloths, with the rose topping the list. In our opinion, nobody captured their realism as well as the Bogdanovich team.

Both Sergei and Tamara were born into the Russian aristocracy. Tamara's father was a General in the Czarist army and a WWI war hero. They immigrated to the U.S. when Tamara was approximately fifteen years old. After graduating #1 in the Russian equivalent of West Point, Sergei served with distinction as a Lt. Colonel in the Czar's army. During the Russian Revolution, he fought with honor in the White Army against the Bolshevik Reds. Forced to choose between leaving the country and being executed by the enemy, he immigrated to the United States in approximately 1925. It was here that he met and married Tamara. Neither Sergei nor Tamara had any formal art education, and neither of them practiced their craft until they arrived in the United States.

The Wilendur floral designs by Tamara and Sergei were a true collaborative effort. Tamara was a well-known floral painter at the time, supplying production art to supply houses that catered to interior decorators and hotel chains. She disliked the technical side of the textile design business, and left it to her talented husband Sergei to turn her watercolors into renderings Weil and Durrse could reproduce onto fabric. Sergei would convert her designs into "paint by number" type charts for Wilendur to follow. At the bottom of these renderings were one inch color swatches of the exact colors to be used in each empty blank, thus insuring an accurate representation of the original design. While *all* of the floral designs produced by the team originated from Tamara's watercolor art, Sergei designed a few non-floral patterns of his own. The designs produced by Tamara and Sergei were patented for them *by Wilendur* in Sergei's name alone, possibly due to the prevailing male-dominated attitude of that period. As yet, we have not found Tamara's name on any design patents. They produced for Weil and Durrse over approximately a ten year period, beginning in the early 1950s. During the late 1950s-early 1960s, they were the *only* designers for the company.

A family friend recalls that their house and studio was filled with their wonderful paintings, primarily watercolors. Sergei and wife Tamara were active in the New York social circles and attended many extravaganzas with duchesses and dukes from Czarist Russia, as well as notable artists such as Salvador Dali and his wife Gala. Sergei is fondly remembered as a gentle, courtly man without a single hint of arrogance or conceit.

Measurements: 17x33 inches
Price Range: $30-$35

Two popular Wilendur patterns by artists Tamara and Sergei Bogdanovich ~ Princess Rose (patent applied for on May 19, 1955) and Royal Rose (patent applied for on October 11, 1952). The Royal Rose can be found in red, yellow, pink, and a scarce blue. Princess Rose commonly came in pink, yellow, and occasionally salmon, blue, and purple.
Measurements: 17x33 inches
Price Range: $30-$35 each

Full view of Marion Dorn Christmas tree towel.

Flecks of shimmering gold dress this festive Christmas tree towel by Marion Victoria Dorn (1899- January 24, 1964). Dorn had an illustrious career as a textile designer. She was born in San Francisco and graduated from Stanford University at only sixteen years old. After living in Paris for four years, she moved to London in 1923 with her spouse, graphic designer Edward McKnight Kauffer. It was during her stay in London that her fame grew as a remarkable artist of hand sculpted, modernistic carpets. Her craft was displayed in some of the best known interiors of the time, including the Queen Mary Ocean Liner and many luxury hotels. In 1940, Marion V. Dorn returned to the United States. She dabbled in other art forms such a mosaics and fabrics and was an accomplished still-life and portrait painter, but nothing would ever eclipse her fame as a carpet designer. Dorn passed away in Tangiers, Morocco on January 28, 1964. Towels by this artist are a scarce find. *From the collection of Lynette Gray of www.MamaWiskas.com.*
Measurements: 17x29 inches
Price Range: $40-$45

Part of the Kate Greenaway series by Leacock. Kate Greenaway (1846-1901) was a brilliant artist and illustrator whose work has had an enduring appeal throughout the decades. Her charming designs captured the blissful innocence of childhood and the beauty of nature, and are as endearing today as they were to the Victorians more than a century ago. In 1946, Leaspun Prints (Leacock) produced a serious of tablecloths and towels commemorating the 100th anniversary of Kate's birth. This towel matches her Cornwall tablecloth pattern and is made from spun rayon and cotton. While not terribly absorbent due to the high rayon content, it makes a delightful table runner.
Measurements: 14x23 inches
Price Range: $35-$40

Chapter 8
Animals

"Don't Count Your Chickens Before They Hatch" ~ adorable towel on a pebble finished cotton with a crochet edge added at each end.
Measurements: 15x27 inches
Price Range: $25-$30

What a proud fellow! This handsome rooster towel is hand printed by Leacock onto pure, absorbent linen. The matching tablecloth is simply extraordinary and highly sought after by collectors.
Measurements: 16x29 inches
Price Range: $25-$30

Lustre Dry kitchen terry towel by Barth & Dryfus of California. The tag brags that it "Dries Sparkle Clean in ½ the Time." Of note, the sewn in label is by Cannon with a note that says "made exclusively for towel decorators."
Measurements: 18x27 inches
Price Range: $20-$25

Darling kittens with big blue eyes and balls of yarn to play with in the borders. This all-linen towel is by Parisian Prints.
Measurements: 16x29 inches
Price Range: $20-$25

"Cock A Doodle Doo, Chicken in a Stew." A farmer stands in the background with a hatchet in his hand. The fabric is textured cotton.
Measurements: 14x25 inches
Price Range: $25-$30

A cute pair of linen towels featuring little birds warbling from their perches atop a flowering vine. Musical notes float above them. One towel is printed in red and black and the other is printed in navy and French blue. Both are unused and in mint condition.
Measurements: 16x32 inches
Price Range: $20-25 each

The next three kitten and puppy towels by Broderie Creations are some of their most popular and command consistently high prices. This one shows a pair of felines playing with plump blue cherries. The pattern came in a variety of fabrics and various colors combinations. This particular towel is of cotton.
Measurements: 15x28 inches
Price Range: $50-55

Cocker Spaniel puppies scamper to climb out of a basket ~ another extremely popular collectible pattern by Broderie. Notice the heavy overprinting in luscious Nile green, red, and yellow…classic design elements of the 1930s.
Measurements: 17x26 inches
Price Range: $50-$55

A favorite of collectors, this Broderie Creations towel features an adorable red Scottie dog with a big blue gingham bow around his neck. Scottish Terriers were originally bred as fierce hunters of foxes and badgers, and are a popular collectible theme. This towel is a linen/cotton blend, but it also came in a cotton and a variety of other colors.
Measurements: 17x27 inches
Price Range: $50-$55

"A Sip for Two" ~ darling conversational towel highlighted by a sweet puppy couple sharing a drink under a colorful umbrella. The design is featured on one end of the towel only. This mint and unused hand printed pattern is not often found in the marketplace.
Measurements: 16x27 inches
Price Range: $35-40

Egrets, deer, penguins, and sea gulls are the subject matter on this petite hand printed linen towel in jadeite green shades by Victory K&B.
Measurements: 12x20 inches
Price Range: $20-$25

Right:
These industrious Scottie dogs are a delight as they help with the household chores. Don't they look cute in their aprons? The first Scottish Terrier was registered with the American Kennel Club in the late 1800s, but the breed experienced a sharp rise in popularity with the election of President Franklin Delano Roosevelt. FDR's pet Scottie, Fala, rapidly found his way into the hearts of Americans and became the most popular pet in presidential history. This mint and unused towel still retains a sewn in label stating it was made by Absorbtex.
Measurements: 16x25 inches
Price Range: $30-$35

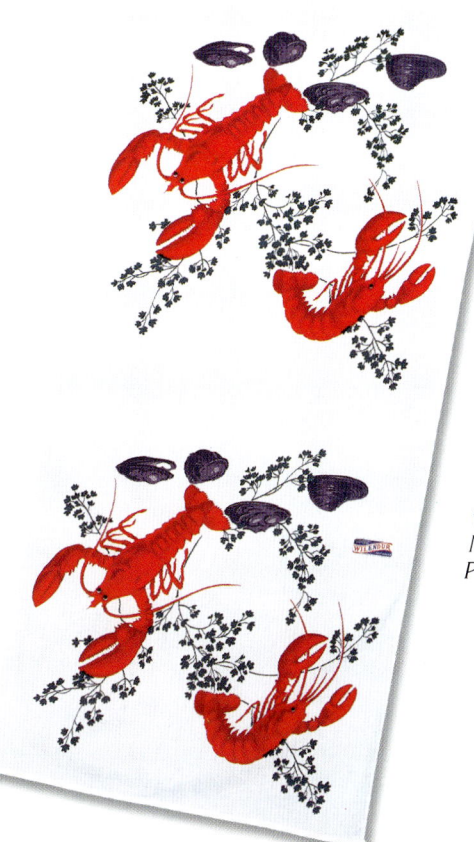

Wilendur lobster and oyster towel with garnishes of parsley. An extremely popular pattern among collectors, this is another fine example of the Bogdanovich design talent. Wilendur's patent application for this pattern was granted on April 1, 1958. It was produced under both the Wilendur (pre 1958) and Wilendure (post 1958) label. Matching tablecloths, aprons, lobster bibs, napkins, and yard goods were also produced. It is a very popular pattern for outdoor clam bakes, despite the fact that these appear to be oysters rather than clams. A paper tagged version of this towel recently sold at auction for nearly $80, although a price that high is a bit unusual.
Measurements: 17x33 inches
Price Range: $45-$50

Butterscotch colored kittens with moss green eyes play happily on this pure Belgian linen towel. A small horse and carriage logo is printed on one corner of the cloth, which tells us this is a Town & Country design.
Measurements: 15x28 inches
Price Range: $30-$35

103

From the maker Parisian Prints (Joseph Sultan and Sons) comes this pair of cute linen cat and dog towels. The pair of towels still retain their original paper tags and a Gimbels price sticker of 2 for $1.00.
Measurements: 16x28 inches
Price Range: $50-$55 pair

Remarkably detailed poodles on luxurious Irish linen by Ulster. Note that the design runs the length of the towel, making it suitable for framing. Be sure to check the manufacturer section in the back of this book for more information about the Ulster Linen Company, Inc.
Measurements: 31x20 inches
Price Range: $20-$25

Playful kittens on this Irish linen towel signed Erinore for Ulster. The original .65 cent price tag is attached. Note that the design runs horizontally rather than vertically. According to Dever Larmor of the Ulster Linen Company, Inc., these horizontal designs were popular for placing flat across a tea tray, but in later years began to be purchased with the sole purpose of framing. Ulster linen towels are of exceptional quality in both fabric and design and are at this time an undervalued vintage collectible. A wise collector would add a few to their stash now while they're still affordable!
Measurements: 30x19 inches
Price Range: $20-$25

Most collectors think "embroidery" when they think of Vogart designs ~ this one is *printed*, but with the words "glasses" artfully embroidered underneath the Art Deco inspired deer design. We initially felt this embroidery might be the result of an innovative and artistic housewife, but have since seen several more of this pattern with the exact same embroidery design. Perhaps it came from the factory this way? Regardless, the combination of print and embroidery makes for a charming towel. *From the collection of Sharon Stark of www.RickRack.com. Photo taken at Butler's Courtyard, League City, Texas.*
Measurements: 15x29 inches
Price Range: $30-$35

"Just Between Us Girls" ~ one can't miss the obvious comparison of the cackling hens to the women chatting in the corners of this pure linen towel. Fabulous 1950s colors of bubblegum pink and aqua with the original paper tag attached.
Measurements: 16x29 inches
Price Range: $25-$30

A subtle, understated design of a proud rooster in bubblegum pink Irish linen damask ~ a reminder that sometimes "less is more." The Hardy Craft Original sticker is still affixed and brags that "nothing dries like linen."
Measurements: 20x30 inches
Price Range: $20-$25

Kitten faces bloom among branches of pussy willow, while puppy faces blossom along with dogwood on this duo of linen towels by Leacock. A very clever theme in wonderful 1950s colors, signed by Martha. As yet, we haven't discovered who Martha is, but our hats are off to her creativity! *Photo taken at Butler's Courtyard, League City, Texas.*
Measurements: 16x29 inches
Price Range: $40-$45 each

Rich, luscious jeweled tones accent a colorful bird on this towel by Wilendur, an elegant departure from their more common "repeating pattern" designs. *Photo taken at Butler's Courtyard, League City, Texas.*
Measurements: 16x27 inches
Price Range: $35-$40

106

Chapter 9

Conversational

"Let's Read the Tea Leaves," designed and signed by Martha and manufactured by Leacock of Canada. This whimsical towel gives instructions on how to "read" tea leaves: *"Pour off all tea and shake the remaining leaves around in the cup. Concentrate on these leaves so that you might decipher their message...allow your fancy to have full play, do not expect to see a realistic picture, a suggestion is sufficient."* Apparently, your fortune and future depend on what you see at the bottom of your cup: a fish means riches, a spider means secrets, and a lamp means joy. The towel is hand printed and made of cotton. *Photo taken at Quakertown Quilts, Friendswood, Texas.*
Measurements: 17x28 inches
Price Range: $30-$35

Full view of "Let's Read The Tea Leaves" towel.

Children's letter blocks towels: A is for apple, B is for berry and also for beef. The original .69 cent price tag and "pure linen" stickers are still affixed.
Measurements: 15x28 inches
Price Range: $25-$30 each

"Cool As A [Cucumber]" ~ one of a series of towels that included various expressions such as "Busy As A Bee" and "Pretty As a Picture."
Measurements: 16x27 inches
Price Range: $25-$30

"Easy as [Pie]" and "Apple Pie and [Coffee]" towel duo in pure linen. Part of a series of food related towels that included such tasty culinary combinations as "Steak and Eggs," "Ham and Beans," and "Tomato and Lettuce." These towels came in cotton and a variety of color combinations.
Measurements: 16x27 inches
Price Range: $25-$30 each

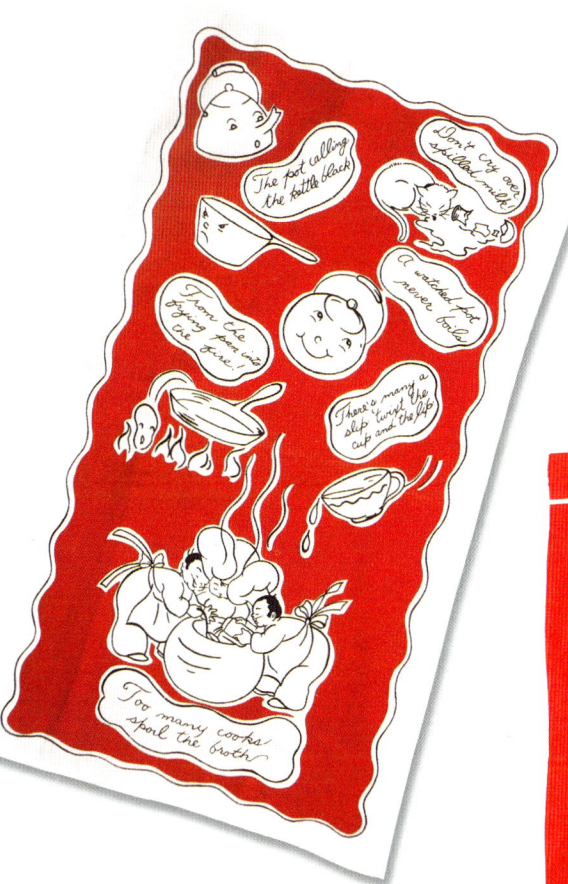

A trio of plump chefs hover over a large pot, spewing forth bits of kitchen wisdom: "Too Many Cooks Spoil the Broth," "Don't Cry Over Spilled Milk," "The Pot Calling the Kettle Black," "From the Frying Pan Into the Fire," and "There's Many a Slip 'Twixt The Cup and the Lip."
Measurements: 15x27 inches
Price Range: $25-$30

Here is an interesting uncut piece of home yard goods: two different designs are printed side by side with a dotted line down the center. The homemaker would cut the pieces apart and hem them into two separate towels.
Price Range: $25-$30

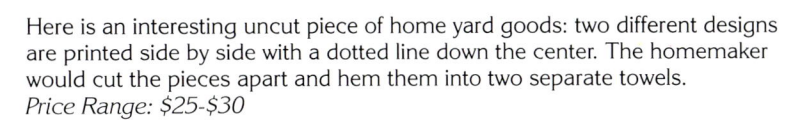

Springerle rolling pin towel from Martex. This specialized type of rolling pin is used to emboss butter cookies with lovely decorative designs, after which the dough is cut apart and baked. The German name springerle means "little knight," possibly because that was a traditional design element on early springerle presses. This "Dry-Me-Dry" towel came in a variety of colors including blue, yellow, green, and red. Be sure to see page 45 for more information on the Dry-Me-Dry fabric.
Measurements: 20x30 inches
Price Range: $25-$30

What's in *your* cupboards? This colorful towel features a variety of colorful foods with brand-name knockoffs of the originals, including "mello" for Jello®, "cisco" for Crisco®, and what looks suspiciously like the Aunt Jemima® and Borden® logos on other packaging.
Measurements: 15x27 inches
Price Range: $35-$40

No well stocked pantry would be found without such essential kitchen staples as catsup, jelly, pears, peas, plums, beats, soup, olives, tea, and corn. Colorful cherries dance across the background of this Leacock Prints towel.
Measurements: 17x28 inches
Price Range: $25-$30

A trio of Sun Glo towels in the Wrought Iron pattern. These towels came in red, green, yellow, turquoise, and pink and are popular with those who love "Eames Era" inspired designs. The husband and wife team of Charles and Ray Eames were groundbreaking designers of Modernistic architectural, industrial, and furniture designs.
Measurements: 17x26 inches
Price Range: $25-$30 each

What's on the shopping list today? Steak, lobster, cheese, and salad ~ my goodness, perhaps company is coming! This graphic conversational towel is by Leacock Prints and is hand printed on heavy cotton.
Measurements: 16x28 inches
Price Range: $20-$25

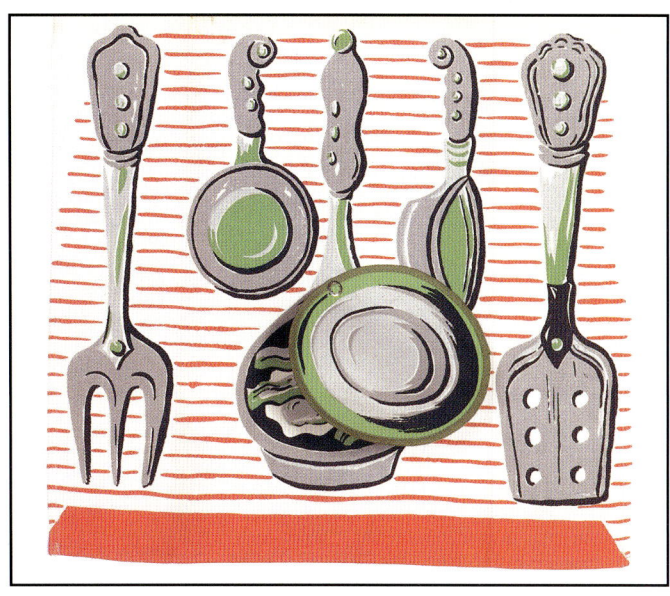

Green eggs and bacon sizzle in the frying pan and the lid snaps off to become a potholder. This clever conversational towel is by Paragon Needlecraft, best known for their embroidery and handwork patterns and supplies. Here is a recipe for you to make your *own* green eggs and ham breakfast, if you're brave enough to try:

1-2 tablespoons of butter
4 slices of ham
8 eggs
2 tablespoons of milk
1-2 drops of green food coloring
¼ teaspoon of salt
¼ teaspoon of pepper

Melt the butter in a large frying pan over medium heat, add sliced ham and brown until edges are slightly crisp. Remove the ham from the pan, cover with foil and set aside. In a medium size mixing bowl, combine the eggs, milk, salt and pepper. Beat with a whisk until frothy. Then add 1-2 drops of green food coloring until you reach the desired shade of green. Heat a tablespoon of butter in a large frying pan over medium heat until the butter begins to sizzle. Then add the egg mixture to the pan. Stir the egg mixture with a spatula until the eggs are firm and not too runny. Transfer eggs to individual plates. Add the ham prepared earlier and garnish with a sprig of parsley.

Measurements: 16x28 inches
Price Range: $25-$30

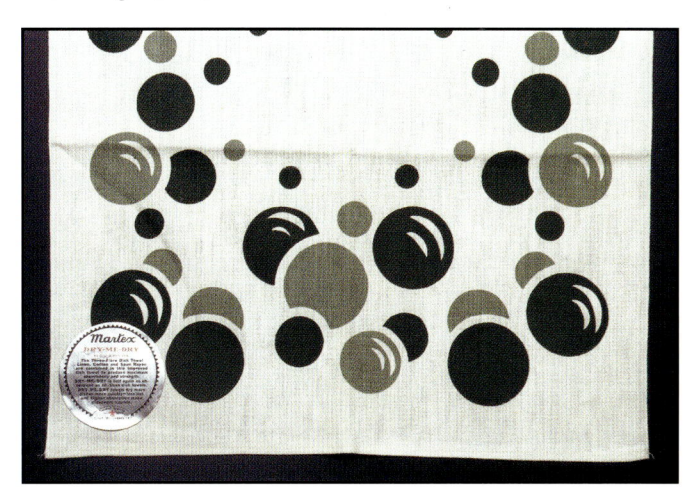

Charming country kitchen shelves cotton towel from Sun Glo. This hand printed piece also came in blue, green, and yellow, and had a matching tablecloth as well.
Measurements: 16x28 inches
Price Range: $20-$25

Bubbles, bubbles, and more bubbles on this Martex Dry-Me-Dry towel! This wonderful three-fiber towel still retains its .29 cent price sticker from Bloomingdale's. It can be found in a variety of colors, including green, blue, red, brown, and yellow.
Measurements: 16x30 inches
Price Range: $20-$25

111

A trio of one-color hand printed linen towels with their original .29 cent price tags from Scranton Dry Goods Company.
Measurements: 17x30 inches
Price Range: $20-$25 each

Left:
A luscious color combination of 1930s green and red on creamy linen.
Measurements: 17x32 inches
Price Range: $20-$25

Right:
There is a decidedly Russian influence on this wonderful samovar towel by Wilendur. Originally a Persian innovation, the samovar came to Russia in the 18th century. Essentially a means by which water is kept heated for tea, the original samovars were heated by wood and could be quite ornate. Modern Russians still embrace this unique Persian device, and electric versions can be found in kitchens, offices, and trains. As for the towel itself, we wonder if this might be a Sergei Bogdanovich design, given his Russian heritage.
Measurements: 15x27 inches
Price Range: $30-$35

Two "Buxom Biddies" spend a busy day together baking a cake, grilling chickens, stirring a pot of soup, flipping pancakes, stopping to chat and knit, mixing (and tasting) a pie crust, and finally carrying the finished pie. Household chores are always much more fun when shared with a cheerful friend!
Measurements: 17x31 inches
Price Range: $30-$35

Tea time! A one-color, hand blocked tea towel by Superior Hand Print of Los Angeles, California. Note that the paper tag refers to CALIF, rather than the current state abbreviation of CA. This dates the towel to a twenty year period between 1943 and 1963, although we suspect the true date is closer to the beginning of that era.
Measurements: 17x28 inches
Price Range: $25-$30

A change from the usual "whimsical people" designs Broderie is best known for ~ this one features decorative plates with tranquil home and town scenes.
Measurements: 15x28 inches
Price Range: $20-$25

A striking two-color design in rich red and blue on a creamy color linen featuring a coffee pot, teapot, cup and plates.
Measurements: 17x29 inches
Price Range: $20-25

Hee Haw! A cute little donkey planter is filled with cacti and a pottery dish overflows with daisies on this whimsical design by Wilendur. This pattern came in a variety of colors, including blue, red, and green.
Measurements: 17x28 inches
Price Range: $30-$35

How do you like *your* eggs? A colorful and clever conversational towel featuring anthropomorphic egg-people with delightfully comical graphics. The hard-boiled egg looks positively villainous, doesn't he?
Measurements: 16x27 inches
Price Range: $30-$35

Until the late 1950s and early 1960s, terry cloth toweling was primarily confined to the bath and beach. The popular printed designs didn't adhere well to terry and the prints were not as crisp and defined as consumers desired. A shame, since terry's absorbent and functional qualities were otherwise quite suitable for the kitchen. These Parisian Prints kitchen towels still have their original tags, proclaiming that their designs have a "French Accent."
Measurements: 17x28 inches
Price Range: $25-$30 set

We think this whimsical towel is simply "eggs-traordinary"! The magician is juggling various kitchen implements and eggs while a confused rabbit watches from the top hat. The border of this delightful Leacock Quality Hand Prints towel shows the many ways one can prepare scrambled eggs.
Measurements: 16x28 inches
Price Range: $25-$30

This Belcrest Linens calorie towel was made in Hong Kong, which may account for the spelling errors ~ "un"chovies, anyone? In comparison to most calorie towels, a gourmet selection of food is found here, including foie gras, caviar, bouillon, and brie. I believe I'll stick with the hamburger and cherry pie, thank you!
Measurements: 16x27 inches
Price Range: $25-$30

An easy way for calorie counters to watch their weight…or at least feel guilty about sneaking into the pantry for a midnight snack. We've noticed that the calorie content of treats varies from towel to towel…so which one are we supposed to believe?
Measurements: 16x29 inches
Price Range: $25-$30

115

Three vintage cards showing serving sizes for various foods ~ possibly used for a nutrition training class.

Fitness guru Jack LaLane brought weight management into the limelight during the 1950s. The number of vintage linens with calorie counting themes attests to the fact that women of previous decades were as concerned with watching their weight as women of today. The whimsical graphics on this vintage towel remind calorie counters what foods are safely allowed, ranging from four calorie mushrooms to bonbons that simply warn "danger."
Measurements: 16x28 inches
Price Range: $25-$30

Modern dieting offers a multitude of options ranging from low carbohydrates to eating nothing but cabbage soup, but forty or fifty years ago it was all about counting calories. As seen, many variations of this theme were produced over a decade or more and they came in a myriad of colors. These three towels bear the Parisian Prints tag, but similar versions of this popular theme were produced by a variety of manufacturers. Tablecloths and even handkerchiefs were also printed in calorie counting themes.
Measurements: 16x29 inches
Price Range: $25-$30

117

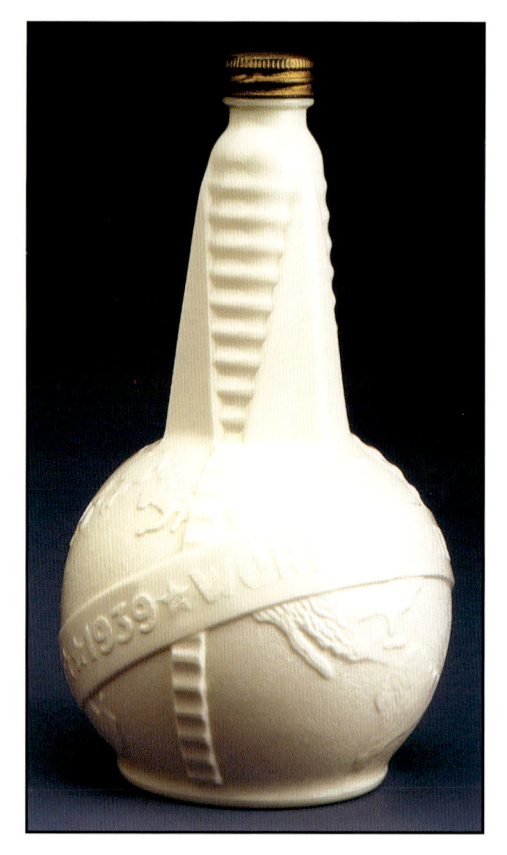

New York 1939 World's Fair by Taylor, Wellington Sears Co. This towel is signed by E. Barton and depicts the Hall of Communications on one end and the administration building on the other.
Measurements: 15x27 inches
Price Range: $60-$65

Souvenir bottle from the Great Atlantic & Pacific Tea Company commemorating the 1939 New York World's Fair ~ at one time this collectible bottle held pure cider vinegar.

A wonderfully abstract rendition of New York City, highlighting the Statue of Liberty in the foreground and the Manhattan skyline behind. One of the most marvelous and enduring gifts ever bestowed on the United States, the Statue of Liberty was sculpted by French artist Auguste Bartholdi. Construction of the massive lady, who was presented to the American people by the people of France, started in 1875 in Paris and was completed in 1884. She was dismantled and shipped to the United States, where she was reassembled on Liberty Island in 1886. Miss Liberty stands an incredible 305 feet from the ground to the tip of her majestic torch. Souvenir towels such as this were popular and inexpensive trinkets to take home from family vacations. Because of the rise in nostalgia for the "good old days," they have become increasingly popular collectibles in recent years.
Measurements: 15x27 inches
Price Range: $50-$55

118

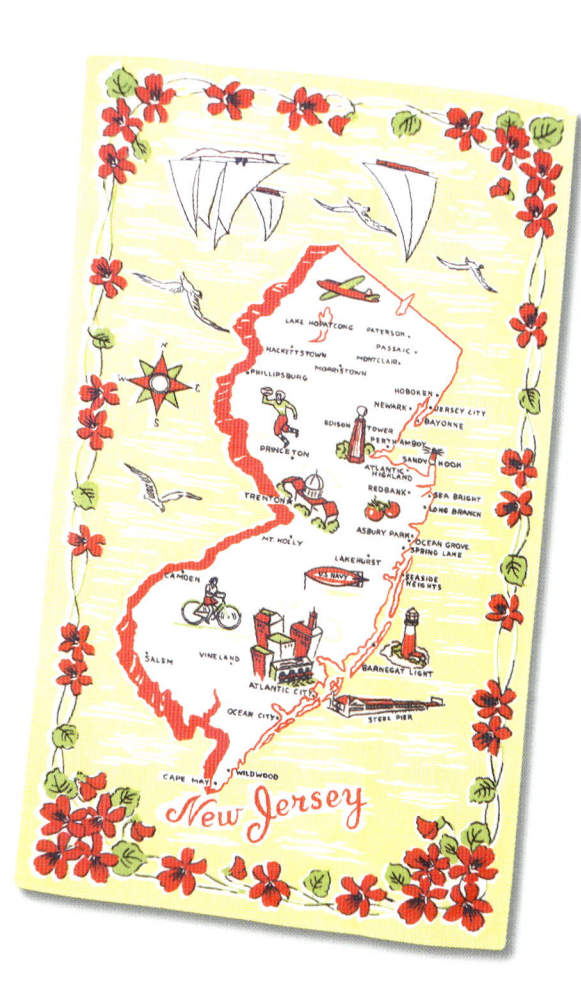

A fab 1950s New Jersey state souvenir towel in sunny yellow with a border of sweet red violets. This hand printed beauty is made of cotton sailcloth.
Measurements: 16x27 inches
Price Range: $40-$45

An Original Yucca Print souvenir towel featuring the state of California. Boulder Dam is depicted, which provides a clue for dating this towel to the 1940s ~ the dam was renamed Hoover Dam in 1947. We must caution you against using the graphics on vintage souvenir textiles as the *only* source of dating, however. We know of several instances regarding both vintage tablecloths and towels where the company continued to print the design for a decade or two after its birth, long after some landmarks had been re-named.
Measurements: 16x26 inches
Price Range: $40-$45

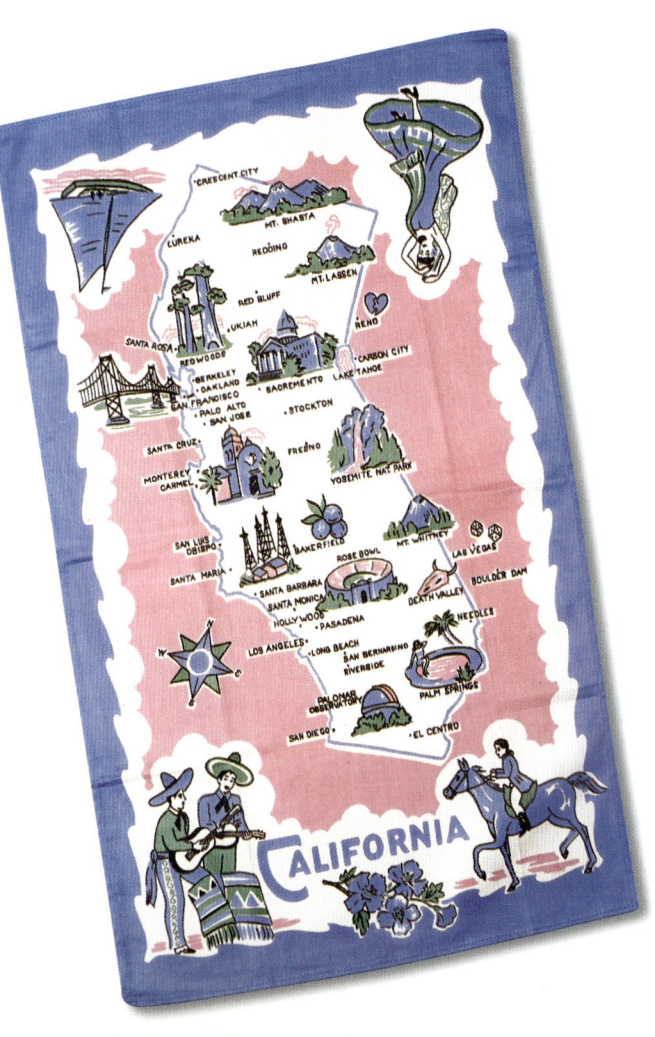

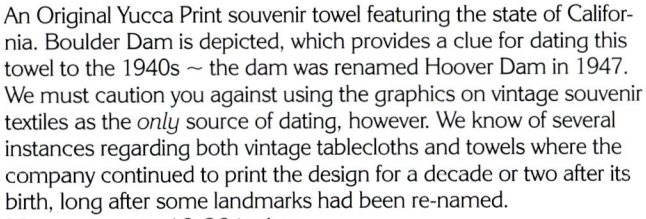

Here is an example of a towel that may have been printed long past its original design date. It depicts a scene of Boulder Dam, renamed Hoover Dam in 1947, yet the color combination is decidedly 1950s. We enjoy finding spelling errors on vintage towels and this one has *two* ~ note the spelling of Sacramento and Bakersfield.
Measurements: 16x28 inches
Price Range: $40-$45

Vintage magazine advertisement for Union Pacific Railroad.

Sunshine State souvenir towel from Miami Originals of Miami, Florida. Towel still retains its .69 cent price tag from Neisner's. This novelty towel features flamingos, palm trees, and a border of oranges, pineapples, fish, and coconuts.
Measurements: 15x26 inches
Price Tag: $40-$45

Fantastic vintage 1950s Florida souvenir cloth featuring vacationing families and couples enjoying the Sunshine State's many amenities: sun bathing, golfing, sailing, water skiing, and just relaxing. This mint condition towel is made of cotton.
Measurements: 15x30 inches
Price Range: $40-$45

California souvenir towel in very 1950s colors of turquoise and pink. A small horse and carriage, the logo for Town & Country linens, is printed in one corner. The most popular tourist destinations during the 1930s to the 1960s were California, Florida, and New York, and as such, souvenir towels from those states are abundantly found in the marketplace.
Measurements: 16x28
Price Range: $40-$45

A souvenir towel from Maine in its original Kay Dee wrappings. Note the similarities of the packaging to the Bestex towel on page 94 ~ the wording on the back side is identical.
Price Range: $30-$35

A hand printed souvenir towel from the maker Sun Glo, featuring a main street market scene of a quaint pastry shop and flower cart. Of note, the flag holding the Sarasota Springs, New York name was ironed on, rather than factory printed. It simply wasn't cost-effective to have a souvenir towel specially printed for a small town or tourist destination. Instead, the manufacturer would ship towels such as this to gift stores across the country, which in turn would iron on their own city logo to create a souvenir towel from that area.
Measurements: 15x38 inches
Price Range: $30-$35

121

Detail of Autumn towel from the set below.

A towel for every season: Spring, Summer, Autumn, and Winter. Different seasonal scenes are depicted on each towel ~ Easter and springtime fun; fishing, golf, tennis, and boating during the summer months; Halloween and Thanksgiving turkey in the fall; sledding and ice skating during the winter. These towels can periodically be found separately, but rarely as a complete set. The fabric is surprisingly lightweight cotton, similar to flour sack.
Price Range: $100-$110 set

122

When Lake Placid businessman, Julian Reiss, told his young daughter a fanciful story of a baby bear visiting Santa Claus at his North Pole workshop, little did he know his daughter's pleas to visit the jolly old elf would be the beginnings of America's oldest theme park. His vision of a "summer residence" for Santa was brought to life by the team of designer/artist Arto Monaco and construction/developer Harold Fortune on the site of Whiteface Mountain, New York. From a small crowd of 212 opening day visitors on July 1, 1949 to a record 14,000 on September 2, 1951, this "New North Pole" attracted a steady stream of visitors. On December 16th, 1953, the U.S. Postal Service awarded it "rural postal station" status, and was no doubt was relieved to finally have a legitimate address to deliver thousands of children's letters to Santa. This Santa's Workshop North Pole souvenir towel still has the original .98 cent price tag attached and is an extremely popular collectible pattern. Matching tablecloths were also sold as souvenirs. If bought or sold during the holiday season, one could easily expect the price to double. *From the collection of Donna Cardwell (www.dcardblueslinencloset.com).*
Measurements: 18x26 inches
Price Range: $40-$45

This unusual Startex Mills Christmas towel is quite an interesting find ~ we speculate that it may have been a gift to its employees or possibly company vendors. The sewn in label states that the fabric content is 65% cotton and 35% linen.
Measurements: 17x30 inches
Price Range: $25-$30

A festive Christmas hostess apron with shimmery gold accents ~ the red portion of the apron is actually a towel, cut in half and sewn onto a creamy linen base. Factory made by Town and Country Linen Company, it could fool you into believing it was a creatively homemade piece.
Price Range: $15-$20

123

Four festive Parisian Prints Christmas towels.
Price Range: $20-$25 each

The graphics on this 1940s-1950s Newlyweds Gift Towel were off-color and risqué by vintage standards, yet items such as this were popular gag gifts of the era. Why the dichotomy between conservative values and this risqué trend? Perhaps it began during World War II with the acceptance of pin-up girls, or maybe it was due to the overnight sensation of Marilyn Monroe's centerfold in the first *Playboy Magazine* (1953). Whatever the reason, towels such as this became acceptable gag gifts for newly married couples. This one might raise an eyebrow or two even today!
Measurements: 15x27 inches
Price Range: $20-$25

Original Willy The Weeper Creation crying towel, "guaranteed to absorb any kind of tears." A whole series of "crying towels" was produced for every occasion ~ there were golfers' crying towels, bowlers' crying towels, vacationers' crying towels, and towels for the miserable husband and much-aligned wife. If you could think up a reason to whine, no doubt Willie the Weeper had beat you to the punch with a towel to absorb your tears. Willie got his name from the 1927 song by Grant V. Rymal, Walter Melrose, and Marty Bloom with the following lyrics:

VERSE 1:
Have you ev-er heard the sto-ry folks of Will-ie the Weep-er?
Wil-lie's oc-cu-pa-tion was a chim-ney sweep-er
He had the dream-in' ha-bit and he had it bad:
Lis-ten and I'll tell you 'bout the dreams he had.
VERSE 2:
He - dreamed he had a barrel of dia-mond rings - and mon-ey,
Mam-mas by the score to love and call him hon-ey,
Ev-'ry-where he went the peo-ple all would say,
"There's the guy who put the 'B' in old Broad-way."
CHORUS:'
Oh, Ba-by, tell me, what would you do,
If you could have all your dreams come true?
There's some-thing tells me, you'd lock the door,
Like Wil-lie the Weep-er, you'd cry for more.
Copyright 1927 Melrose Music Corp

Measurements: 16x27 inches
Price Range: $20-$25

"How Old Are *You*?" A suggestive, risqué towel that would have been given as a gag gift to a male friend, hopefully one with a good sense of humor. Look at the bulls' tails…need we say more???
Measurements: 17x26 inches
Price Range: $20-$25

While the chef sleeps, the vegetables strike up the band. This comical anthropomorphic towel is from Society Creations and hand printed onto linen fabric.
Measurements: 16x27 inches
Price Range: $25-$30

125

One of our all-time favorites from a series of Irish linen towels featuring anthropomorphic fruit. We've nicknamed this one the "death march of lemons" or the "sadistic lemonade" towel. The closer they get to the woman making lemonade, the more sour the look on their faces become. And did you notice the calendar on the wall? It's Friday the 13th! The series included an orange and pear theme (also featured here) as well as others with apples, cherries, and raspberries.
Measurements: 23x31
Price Range: $50-$55

SHHHHH…don't wake the sleeping pears! Another cute anthropomorphic Irish linen towel from a series that includes oranges, raspberries, lemons, cherries, and apples. This one highlights pears sleeping blissfully on a drying rack. Coming to their rescue is a bluebird with a twig who tries to tickle a pear awake and a spider carrying eight little cups of water to rehydrate the dreaming fruit. There is even a worm diving down from the light fixture trying to come to the rescue of the poor unsuspecting pears before they are dried to death. We can't help but wonder why these critters didn't try to rescue the poor lemons on the "sadistic lemonade" towel!
Measurements: 23x31 inches
Price Range: $50-$55

Another from our favorite anthropomorphic towel series. The housemaid here is once again being somewhat sadistic with her fruit ~ this time she peels the poor oranges, only to leave them shivering naked in the cold. As with all the towels in this series, it is made from Irish linen and is oversized. *From the collection of Dr. Christine Dickinson.*
Measurements: 23x31 inches
Price Range: $50-$55

1907 Tuck and Sons anthropomorphic postcard from the Garden Patch Series.

Flip this whimsical towel one way and you have smiling veggies, forks, teapot, and plate ~ turn it the other direction and you've got a plate crying its eyes out. This colorful towel came in a variety of colors including red, blue, yellow, and green.
Measurements: 15x28 inches
Price Range: $25-$30

This darling "java man" is pouring himself a cup of…*himself*??? A cute red polka dot ruffle is attached to the bottom of the towel and the design is on one end only. *Measurements: 16x25 inches*
Price Range: $60-$65

Broderie donkey and anthropomorphic veggie cart towels in two colors.

128

1956 Jello® gelatin advertisement.

Pat-a-cake, pat-a-cake, baker's man.
Make me some Jell-O as fast as you can.
Pick a new flavor and mold it in shape---
Black Raspberry, Black Cherry, or delicious new Grape.

Precious anthropomorphic gelatin-man towel in heavy cotton. The whimsical design by Bucilla is framed by a border of dancing cherries. *Photo taken at Butler's Courtyard, League City, Texas.*
Measurements: 16x28 inches
Price Range: $45-$50

129

Chefs' faces dancing on picks sticking into tomatoes with a bowl of steaming tomato soup at the top of the towel. This towel is made from heavy cotton and is another darling design by Bucilla. *Photo taken at Butler's Courtyard, League City, Texas.*
Measurements: 16x28
Price Range: $45-$50

These anthropomorphic fruits and veggies don't seem to mind that they're about to become dinner as they dance in a ring around the lady of the house pondering over her cookbook. But isn't that what we love so much about anthropomorphic items in general? No matter what their fate, they usually seem to take it all in stride. *Photo taken at Butler's Courtyard, League City, Texas.*
Measurements: 16x28 inches
Price Range: $45-$50

Acquisition, Cleaning, and Storage

Acquisition

Colorful kitchen towels of the 1930s to the 1960s are affordable, collectible, and relatively easy to obtain. Garage sales, estate sales, antique shops, and flea markets are all good sources, as are reputable Internet web sites. (Some online sources we've happily purchased from are listed in the resource guide at the back of this book.) The prices will vary based largely on condition and design ~ as with any vintage textile, be prepared to pay more if the towel is unused, boasts a designer name, or has a particularly popular pattern.

Arming yourself with as much information as possible will help you grow your vintage textile collection grow into a fine one. For example, one tidbit of information we had suspected for years was confirmed for us during the research of this book: We had often wondered why there are such variations on the hems of tea towels. Why do some have four hems and others only two? Why do we often see three hems with one side selvedge? Did this have something to do with towels that are hemmed at home versus store bought towels? Tea towels (and print tablecloths) made of home yard-goods fabric do not generally hold the same value as store-bought ones, so answering that question is an important one for the collector. Unfortunately, the answer is an ambiguous "it varies." When printing toweling, it was more cost-effective for the converting mill to print a *wide* width of fabric, cut it into long strips, and hem the cut sides. Using this method, the middle pieces of the fabric would be hemmed on all four sides, while the outside strips would often show three hems and a side selvedge. A more expensive printing and finishing method would be to run narrower strips the width of the finished product and simply hem the short ends. The ultimate choice would lie in the hands of the company purchasing the finished product.

Before purchasing a towel, ask yourself what purpose it will serve. If you plan on subjecting it to daily use and abuse in the kitchen, then fading, minor spotting, or a tiny hole may be acceptable. If its primary function is to serve as a display piece or to hold onto in hopes of its value appreciating (we've seen a marked rise in prices over the past couple of years), then we suggest you consider mint condition items, preferably unused. Having a paper tag attached is an added bonus. Keep in mind that damage, stains, or fading will significantly lower the value of any vintage textile. Knowing your own level of perfection is important ~ only *you* know what flaws you can live with!

Cleaning

This towel is truly *filthy* from sitting in a storage drawer for the past fifty years. The center area is especially soiled from coming into contact with wood acid at the bottom of the drawer and the whole towel is covered in a brownish glaze from improper storage.

Fortunately, 99% of the soiling was easily removed with only a thirty minute soak using the cleaning methods described in this chapter. We were satisfied with the results and decided not to risk fading by trying remove the *tiny* bit of fold-line discoloration that still remains. *Always* quit when you are satisfied ~ attempts to remove tiny imperfections could result in fading, which can seriously reduce the value of your towel.

Yvonne cleans and restores vintage linens daily for her Internet business, FineVintageLinens.com, so it's no small matter when she claims this Wilendur Wild Rose towel to be one of the nastiest, filthiest pieces she's ever run across! Fifty years contact with wood acid combined with layer upon layer of cigarette smoke covered the entire towel in a heavy brown glaze. She bought two identical towels in the same nasty condition, one to leave as an example of "before" and the other to wash. Could she get it clean???

Of course she could! This one took more attention than most and multiple changes of the soaking water as it turned a disgusting brown color, but in only two or three hours the towel sparkled. There is just a *very* slight fade to the design, but we consider this well-rescued.

An improperly stored textile can look like an ancient relic, while a well kept piece can be pristine. We recommend that you clean your towels as soon as reasonably possible after purchasing. Some collectors will argue that a vintage towel retaining its original paper tags should not be cleaned. If you plan on reselling it at a later date, we agree, since any fading will lower the resale value. However, if the cloth is to remain a permanent part of your collection, taking time to properly clean and store it will extend its life by decades.

Every textile lover has a favorite method of stain removal. We have tested hundreds of cleaning concoctions with many successes and some disasters. The methods and products described here have repeatedly proven to be relatively safe for vintage fabrics, but keep in mind that there are no guarantees a sixty-year-old stain can be safely removed. *These cleaning tips are not necessarily the best choice for other types of textiles, such as silk, embroidery, or quilts.*

Always start with the gentlest cleaning method and work you way up if the stains persist. If at any time during the cleaning process you are satisfied with the results of your efforts, **stop**! Rinse the fabric thoroughly and move on to the storage section below. Remember, some stains will never disappear completely and continual efforts to remove a particularly stubborn spot will only result in fading or damage to the cloth.

It is a good idea to gather a few basic supplies before you begin the cleaning process. We recommend the following:

• Liquid Ivory Snow® or any gentle pH balanced liquid dish soap without fancy scents. The cheapest store brands work well.

• Rubber gloves to protect your hands from the cleaning chemicals.

• A large plastic tub, five gallons or larger, for soaking. Various sizes can be found in the storage section of your favorite discount store. Never soak in metal containers.

• A long handled plastic spoon for stirring your towels.

• Any sodium percarbonate based cleaner *with no optical brighteners or fillers*. We prefer a product called Oxy Boost™ (see resource guide).

• Any quality laundry detergent *with no optical brighteners*. We favor Oxy Prime™ (see resource guide)

- Any quality pre-wash stain treatment spray. We have had great results with many Carbona® products and especially like their Stain Wizard™ pre-wash. Zout® pre-wash is another good choice.

- For rust, our hands-down favorite product is Magica Rust Remover in the spray or gel form (see resource guide). Carbona also makes a good product for rust removal.

A word about chlorine bleach: ***don't***. We do not recommend the use of chlorine bleach in cleaning *any* vintage textile. It can cause devastating damage to the fibers of the cloth. You may not see the results immediately, but several washes down the road you will regret your decision to use it. Similarly, we do not recommend you use a washing machine or dryer. The agitating and tumbling motion can lead to small holes in the cloth.

Surprisingly, one of the safest and most effective methods of cleaning vintage textiles is also the least expensive. Crofting, or grass bleaching, has been a favored method of stain removal and whitening for centuries. Simply laying wet linens out on a green lawn on a sunny day will remove many stubborn stains naturally. Start by soaking your towel in a solution of 1/4 cup liquid Ivory Snow for each five gallons of warm water. Stir it often and watch for signs of dye running into the water. Remove the cloth immediately if bleeding occurs. After a 24-48 hour soak, rinse thoroughly; the rinse water should be crystal-clear and clean enough to drink. Roll the item in a clean terrycloth towel (jelly roll style) or gently squeeze excess water from the cloth (never wring or twist). Lay the cloth flat on a sunny green lawn while still damp. As the oxygen released from the grass passes through the damp fabric, a chemical reaction occurs which will whiten and remove stains. Turn the item over to sun both sides equally, re-dampening with a light mist from a spray bottle or garden hose if necessary. Occasionally, a second day in the sun is needed.

Of course, not everybody has access to a green lawn on a sunny day, or perhaps your degree of time and patience requires a "quick fix." In this case, there are several chemical products that are effective. Since we use Oxy Boost and Oxy Prime almost daily with excellent results, our instructions are based upon those products. If you choose a different cleaning product make sure it does not contain optical brighteners, which are essentially invisible dyes that cling to the fibers and are difficult to rinse clean. Many products on the grocery store shelves contain optical brighteners ~ if in doubt, contact the manufacturer before use. As with any chemical, be sure to heed any manufacturer's warnings and wear rubber gloves to protect your hands. Inhaling any chemical product should be avoided, so use these products in a well ventilated area. It is ***extremely*** important that you do not soak textiles with rayon, silk, or wool fibers, metallic gold, or metallic silver accents in any sodium percarbonate product. This chemical can have an adverse reaction with those types of textiles and severe damage can occur. Sadly, we have a pile of ruined vintage linens to prove this point! A long soak in Liquid Ivory Snow is a safe alternative.

Start by spot treating any food stains with a good pre-wash stain treatment and allow it to work for twenty minutes prior to soaking. If you chose to use the Oxy Boost/Oxy Prime combination, we have found that a smaller amount of the product than specified on their label can be used and still produce marvelous results (three ounces of Oxy Boost plus one ounce of Oxy Prime for each five gallons). Dissolve both of the Oxy chemicals thoroughly in hot water, then add enough lukewarm water until it reaches bathtub temperature. Swishing and stirring often, allow the cloth to soak while checking the progress frequently. Remove it as soon as you are satisfied with the results. A two hour soak is generally ample for simple storage stains…occasionally as little as five or ten minutes is all that is needed. Heavy storage marks or food stains may require a longer bath. Soaking longer than necessary can result in unnecessary fading, so don't over-do it! *Rinse thoroughly* until the water is crystal clear, then roll the item up in a clean terrycloth bath towel to remove excess water. At the risk of sounding like a broken record, laying the cloth flat on your green lawn is the ideal way to dry it. If a lawn is not available, drape a clean terry towel over a door or shower rod and spread the cloth neatly on top to dry.

Storage

If only our grandmothers knew how simple it was to properly store and preserve textiles for future generations, much of our cleaning and restoration efforts would be unnecessary! There are five major causes of damage to textile fibers: prolonged exposure to sunlight, contact with wood acid, detergent or starch left in the cloth, moisture or humidity, and damage along the fold lines. Fortunately, all of these problems can be easily avoided.

Sunlight: Prolonged exposure to sunlight can lead to uneven fading, dry rot, and yellowing. A few hours on the lawn while crofting is fine, but once you're done, store the cloth away from the sun's harmful rays.

Wood Acid: Simply put, wood acid or wood pulp will eat up textiles. Never store your towels directly on a wood surface or in regular tissue paper. Wrap them in several layers of acid free tissue (available from specialty paper stores or dozens of Internet dealers) or unbleached muslin that has been washed and rinsed thoroughly.

Detergent and Starch: This is probably the most common cause of damage to vintage textiles. *Every trace* of detergent must be completely removed from the fabric before storing. Failure to do so will result in that nasty age yellowing that is a common sight for collectors. The rinse water should run crystal clear and be clean enough to drink. Never starch your linens prior to storage. It, too, will cause yellowing and will attract tiny bugs that nibble at the starch and eat little holes in the fabric.

Moisture and Humidity: We can't control the climate we live in, but we can reduce its harmful effects on our colorful tea towels. Make sure your textiles are *completely* dry before tucking them away to avoid brown speckling, mold, and mildew. Avoid storing them in extreme temperatures such as in attics, garages, or basements. *Never* store textiles in plastic. As the temperature fluctuates in your home, condensation will build up inside the plastic over time and lead to mold, mildew, and brown spots. Additionally, there is some recent concern about the chemicals used in plastic leaching out over time and adversely affecting the textile fibers.

Damage along fold lines: Areas of creases or folds become weak at a faster rate than other areas. The ideal way to store textiles is flat, with no folds or creases. Rolling your cloth up in a piece of acid free tissue (jelly roll style) reduces fold lines, as does hanging it. If yours are stored folded, take them out periodically and refold in a different direction each time.

Above all, enjoy your beautiful tea towels! They are versatile and can be a delightful addition in the kitchen or powder room, or used as table runners. Use them to line the bread basket at special family meals. Roll them up and stuff a wicker basket full for a profusion of color. Frame your favorites to hang in the kitchen as colorful works of art. They were made to be admired and *used*. With our knowledge of proper cleaning and storage techniques, these towels can be safely enjoyed for decades to come. You are the caretaker for these beautiful pieces of textile art. With proper care, you can ensure that future generations can enjoy and cherish these bright pieces of history.

Manufacturers

A bonanza of research information is available on the Internet if you have the desire to learn more about the manufacturer of your printed textiles. Much of the information in this section was found on the United States Patent and Trademark Office web site (www.uspto.gov) using their TESS system (trademark electronic search system). Other information was taken from the Federal Trade Commission web site (www.ftc.gov/bcp/rn/). Some of the terminology used here may sound foreign to you, but since it is standard trademark filing text we wanted to include it as found. "Claim in use" refers to the date the manufacturer began using the name in business and often precedes the registration date. A "live" name is still legally owned by the manufacturer, while a "dead" name has either expired or has been cancelled by the manufacturer. When searching for trademark information on TESS, try various names if your initial search yields no results. For example, "Wilendure" can be found by searching the owner's names, Weil and Durrse. For many of manufactures listed below, you will find beginning dates of use, but no ending date. Oftentimes that information is simply not available, and for the sake of accuracy we preferred to leave the dates open ended. Factual information is far preferable over a "guestimate!" Use care in your search and do not mistake a tardy registration date or a renewal as the date the trademark died or expired.

Some manufacturer information is elusive ~ we have searched years for information on many of the thousands of textile manufacturers without uncovering even the slightest morsel of fact. The TESS and FTC search is a rewarding way to date your favorite textiles ~ we encourage you to log on and have fun!

Vintage stereograph showing the weaving room of a cotton mill in South Carolina.

A&S, Abraham & Straus, Inc. Brooklyn, New York. Tablecloths, napkins, doilies, towels, cotton piece goods, textile table tops, wash rags, and handkerchiefs. Claim in use since 1893. Trademark number 492,880 which is now dead. Abraham & Straus continued to produce items under other trademark numbers through the 1986.

America's Pride, Weil & Durrse, Inc. Corporation, New York. Tablecloths, towels, napkins, and toweling. First use April 1, 1941. Filed with USPTO January 31, 1962. Trademark name is now dead.

Aristocraft-Callaway Mills Corporation, La Grange, Georgia. Tablecloths were produced with the Aristocraft tag but the cloths had the famous Callaway signature on one corner. See Callaway Mills.

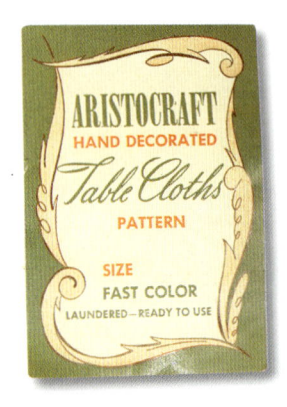

Bates, Bates Manufacturing Company, Inc., Maine. Best known for their chenille bedspreads, Bates also produced table linens. 1949–present. Also produced tablecloths under the **Heirloom** label from 1950-1970.

Belcrest Prints and Belcrest Linens, Belcrest Linens, Corporation, New York. An importer and wholesaler. Tablecloths, towels, and napkins.

Bestex Hand Prints. See Kay Dee.

Bloomingdale's, Bloomingdale Brothers, Inc., New York. For tablecloths, towels, napkins. Claim in use since June 1, 1939.

Boott Mills, Lowell, Massachusetts. A historic company with a rich history, Boott Mills is one of the oldest mill yards in the United States and the buildings (circa 1830s) are the only surviving examples of mill architecture still standing in Lowell. The company was formed in 1835 and continued to expand on its original site through 1956, in spite of being restricted by the boundaries of the Eastern Canal and Merrimack River. Textile production at Boott Mills continued from the 1830s to 1956, when it was finally closed down and the facilities rented out to several small-scale manufacturers and commercial firms. See the resource guide in the back of this book for information regarding the Lowell Textile Museum.

Broderie Creations, A.R. Rosenthal, Inc., New York. An importer, wholesaler, and manufacturer. RN#15937.

136

Bucilla Hand Prints, Bernhard Ulmann Co., Inc., New York, New York. Piece goods of cotton, linen, silk, artificial silk, wool, or combinations thereof; toweling, towels and tablecloths. According to the TESS website, Bucilla's name was first officially issued for use in 1913 and is still active today. The Bucilla name is an abbreviated version of **B**ernhard **U**lmann Company, Inc. Lace, Linen, and Accessories. Originally founded in 1867 by European immigrant Berhard Ulmann, Bucilla has switched owners several times over the years (including an ownership buy out by the long arms of the Indian Head conglomerate) and is currently owned by Plaid Enterprises.

Burlington Industries, Inc., Burlington, North Carolina. Founded in 1923 by J. Spencer Love, Burlington Mills was named for Burlington, N.C., where the first textile plant was completed in 1924. Love experimented with new fabrics including synthetic fiber rayon, which eventually led Burlington to become the largest U.S. producer of rayon fabrics. He acquired many a competitor's mill during the Depression and had 22 plants by the end of 1936. By 1955, Burlington Mills had 17 companies under its umbrella and operated over 100 plants. Its name was changed that year to Burlington Industries. Love continued to guide the company until 1962 when he passed away. According to Burlington's website, they were the first textile company to advertise on network television in 1952 and the first to reach a billion in sales in 1962.

Bur-Mil, Burlington Mills Corporation, Greensboro, North Carolina. Piece goods of wool, cotton, synthetic fibers, and combinations thereof, including tablecloths. Claim in use since 1940, first renewal in 1970. Trademark is now dead.

Calaprint, D.B. Fuller and Co., Inc., New York. Textile fabrics in the piece of cotton, rayon, and mixtures. Claim in use since 1946. Renewed in 1968. Trademark is now dead.

California Hand Prints, California Hand Prints, Inc., Hermosa Beach, California. Tablecloths, luncheon sets, towels, all hand printed. First use in commerce 1936, registered in 1949 and renewed in 1969. Trademark is now dead. Two other labels produced by CHP, **Tropical Hand Prints,** claim in use since February 1944, and **Hawaiian Hand Prints,** claim in use since February 1944.

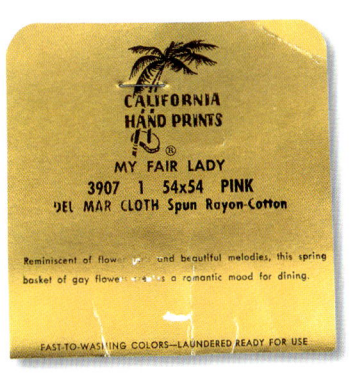

Callaway Mills, Callaway Mills Corporation, La Grange, Georgia. Piece goods of cotton, and of cotton and rayon. First use 1944. Trademark is now dead. Callaway made other textiles prior to 1944, but its trademark claim to tablecloths began in 1944.

Cannon, Cannon Mills Co., Kannapolis, North Carolina. For towels and toweling, sheets and sheeting, tablecloths and napkins. Claim in use since 1916, trademark number 73153390. Kannapolis was founded in 1906 by industrialist James William Cannon. The mill(s) would prosper and grow under his son Charles and would become a household name and the world's largest producer of household textiles. At its apex, the Mills employed some 25,000 people. The Cannon's "mill village" comprised some 1500 homes surrounding the mill. Employees were offered low rent and an assortment of amenities. Cannon Mills and Fieldcrest Mills merged in 1985 after financier David Murdock acquired Cannon. Today, Fieldcrest Cannon is a part of the Pillowtex Corporation and employs approximately 5000 people.

Century Loom, New York Merchandise Co., New York. For tablecloths and napkins made of cotton and rayon fabrics both in the plain and damask weaves. Claim in use in 1940.

Charm Prints, Columbus-Union Oilcloth Company. First use 1929, last renewal in 1969. Produced oilcloth tablecloths until the 1940s, at which time they began producing printed tablecloths. Trademark is now dead.

Cohama, Cohn-Hall-Marx Co., New York. Piece goods of cotton, rayon, and/or silk or combinations thereof. Claims in use since November 15, 1925.

Colonial Hand Prints. See Hollywood Hand Prints.

Color-fornia, California Piece Dye Works, Los Angeles, California. Tablecloths, napkins, and towels. Claim in use since December 1940.

Dunmoy, Stevenson & Son Limited Liability Company, Dungannon, Northern Ireland. Household textile goods, namely tablecloths, placemats, napkins, glass cloths, tea cloths, tray cloths, table runners, and cocktail cloths. Claim in use first in 1953, renewed in 1974, and is now dead.

Dewan, Edmond Co., Fifth Avenue, New York. Textiles by Dewan are usually signed "Styled By Dewan" in a corner of the cloth and the signature is often mistaken as "Styled By Dervan." Artists Carrie Wilson and Mary Sarg were two well-known designers for Dewan.

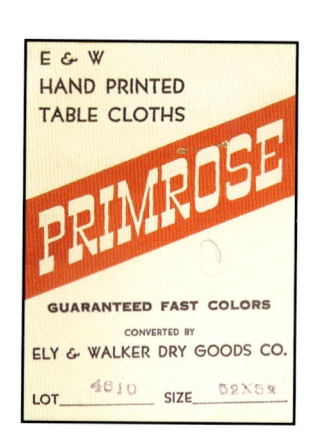

E&W, Ely, Walker and Company Dry Goods, Saint Louis, Missouri. First use 1906, last renewal in 1979. Tablecloths, napkins, bedspreads, handkerchiefs, sheets, pillowcases. Former President George Bush is the great grandson of St. Louis businessman David Davis Walker, and President George Walker Bush is his great-great grandson. D.D. Walker began his textile career as an office boy with a local wholesale dry goods house. He became a partner after only eight years and by 1880 he formed Ely, Walker & Co with Frank Ely. The company became the leading wholesaler of dry goods west of the Mississippi. Other tags under **E&W** were **Brentmoore**, in use from 1921; **Foxcroft**, in use since 1905; **Gilbrae**, in use since 1930; and **La Rhumba**, in use since 1941. All E&W trademarks are dead.

E/S Colorama by Prints Charming. See Prints Charming.

Edsonart, Edson Incorporated Corporation, Chicago, Illinois. Card table covers and piece goods of cotton, linen, and synthetic fibers. Claim first in use in 1944, renewed in 1974, and is now dead.

Everfast, Everfast Fabrics, Inc., New York, New York. Tablecloths, napkins, and tablemats. Claim first in use in 1921 and registered in 1962. It is now dead.

Exclusive. See Joseph Sultan and Sons.

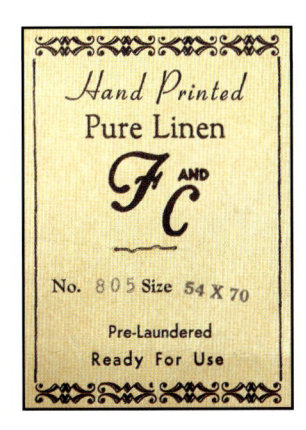

Fallani&Cohn, Fallani & Cohn, Inc., New York, New York. Tablecloths, placemats, towels, and napkins. Several designer names were produced by F&C including Luther Travis, Tammis Keefe, and Martin & Lorraine Ryan (The Ryans). F&C produced under several labels, including Falspun, Falflax, and Faltex.

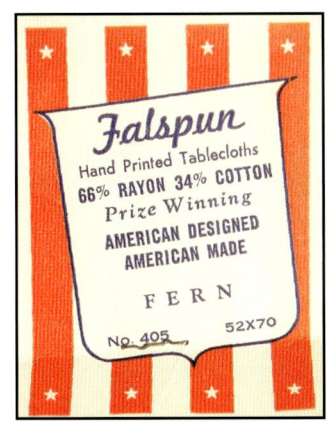

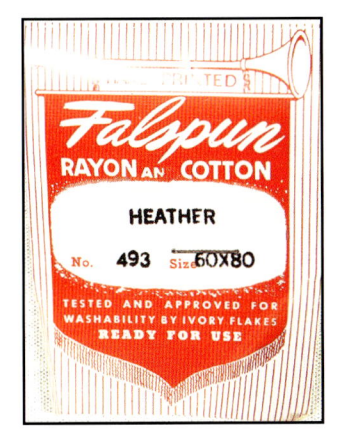

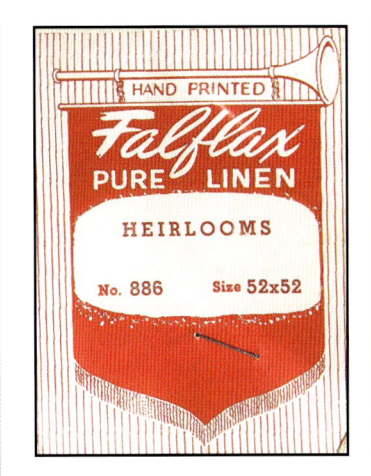

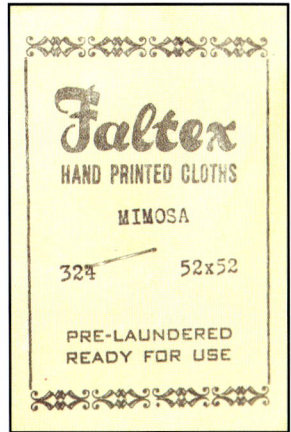

Fashion Manor, J.C. Penney's Co., New York. Cotton and/or rayon piece goods including tablecloths, towels, and toweling. Claim in use since September 1941. See also Pennicraft.

The Fiatelle Co, New York, New York. For cotton and rayon piece goods. Claims in use since April 1, 1929. The Fiatelle name can be found printed on tablecloths with various tags, including Sears Harmony House.

139

Fieldcrest (now Fieldcrest/Cannon). Name first used in 1918, filed with USPTO on November 13, 1941. In the late 1800s, an industrial tycoon named Benjamin Franklin Mebane purchased six hundred acres of land near what is now known as Eden, North Carolina with the ambitious plan of developing it into a textile mill. In 1910, a recession forced him to sell his mills and property to Marshall Fields and Company, who renamed the facilities Fieldcrest Mills. The operation continued to expand and prosper. In 1919, Mr. Fields built another mill in Fieldale, Virginia with an entire community growing up around the mill. In 1953, the Fieldcrest Mills became Fieldcrest, Inc. In 1986, Fieldcrest bought Cannon Mills, forming Fieldcrest Cannon, Inc.

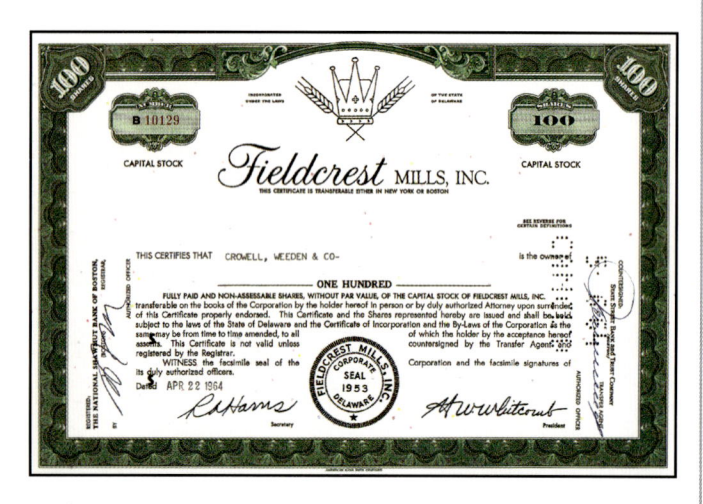

First Lady, Mercantile Stores, Company, Inc., Wilmington, Delaware. Tablecloths, towels, Turkish towels, and printed dish towels. Claim first in use in 1935 and renewed in 1979. Claim is now dead.

Fruit of the Loom, Fruit of the Loom, Inc. Providence, Rhode Island. For cotton and rayon textile piece goods. Claim in use since 1891. One of the few old textile companies that has not only survived but *thrived* over the past century. The founders, brothers Benjamin and Robert Knight, bought their first mill in 1852 and added a new mill every few years afterward, along with the village surrounding the mill. The Knight brothers had a unique knack for rescuing outdated mills from bankruptcy and converting them into modern operations that thrived and turned a large profit. Arguably, a large portion of their success has been credited to the highly popular brand name they adopted in 1887. According to one account, Robert Knight was visiting the home of a friend when he chanced to view a canvas of a rich, golden apple that the daughter of his host had painted. Knight was so impressed with her art that he decided on the spot that it would be used on his company label. More of her paintings were commissioned to be used as brand labels for the many products his factories produced. Various slogans were tried and rejected, but by the 1893 Chicago World's Fair, *all* of the labels had become a standardized bowl of fruit with the "Fruit of the Loom" logo underneath.

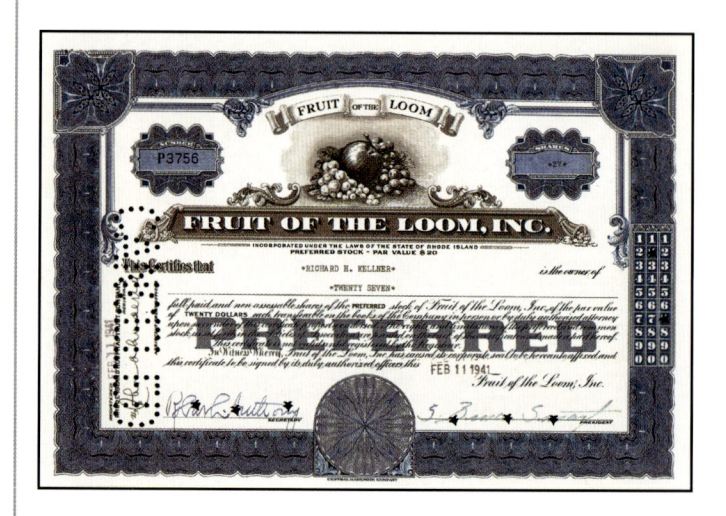

Fruitana, Marvel Linen Corporation, New York. For tablecloths, napkins, tray cloths, doilies. Claim in use since May 1941.

140

Garden State House of Prints, 200 Madison Avenue, New York. Importer, wholesaler, and manufacturer, RN#21641. Prominent designers of the decade were part of the Garden State design team, including Tom Lamb, a well-known handkerchief designer. Also produced with the Garden State Table Toppers & Garden State Creation tag.

Gribbon's, Gribbon Company, Inc. Corporation, New York, New York. Fabrics in the piece of flax, ramie, cotton, and combinations thereof, including plain and embroidered linen, toweling, and damask. First in use in 1923 and last renewed in 1968. Claim is now dead.

Happy Home, F.W. Woolworth Co. Corporation, New York, New York. Tablecloths and curtains. Claim first in use in 1957 and last renewed in 1978. Claim is now dead.

Hardy Craft, James G. Hardy and Co., Corporation. New York, New York. Tablecloths, napkins, runners, and doilies. 1938–present with the Hardy Craft tag *without* the paint palette on its logo.

Hardy Craft Originals, James G. Hardy and Co., Corporation. Tablecloths, napkins, runners, and doilies. Claim in use since 1941 with the Hardy Craft tag *with* the paint palette on its logo. Trademark is now dead.

Hardy Tex, James G. Hardy and Co., Corporation. Tablecloths, napkins, table runners, doilies, place mats, bedspreads, towels, bath mats and bath rugs, draperies, blankets, sheets, pillowcases. First use 1939–present.

Harmony House, Sears Roebuck & Co., Chicago, Illinois. Tablecloths, linens, and towels. Claim in use since 1940.

Hico Master Prints, Hedaya Importing Co., New York. For tablecloths, napkins, doilies. Claim in use since November 5, 1942.

Hollywood Hand Print, D. N. & E. Walter & Co., San Francisco, California. For textile fabric piece goods having hand printed designs thereon; of cotton materials. Claim in use since October 1941. Also produced under the Colonial Hand Print label.

141

Indian Head Mills, Inc. One of the oldest and most recognizable names in textile history, Indian Head cloth is known for its superb quality and was used by numerous textile manufacturers in the production of their finished products. At one time it was said that Indian Head sheeting was used by housewives in every civilized country in the world. In 1916, Indian Head Mills geared up for WWI as half of their output was needed for war use. Once again during WWII, their cloth production shifted from home goods to war needs. The company's advertisements in 1945-46 stated "New supplies of Indian Head will be ready as soon as war restrictions are lifted," and "You will be glad you waited for Indian Head cloth." Indian Head quality was a strong selling point ~ Broderie and Queen Anne (among others) proudly boasted on their paper labels when Indian Head cloth was used.

JS&S, Joseph Sultan and Sons, 40th Street, New York. Importer, wholesaler, manufacturer. See also Exclusive, Parisian Prints, and Sultan Creations.

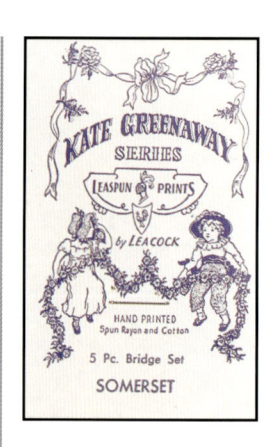

Kate Greenaway Series, Leaspun and Company (Leacock), New York. Produced a series of tablecloths in 1946 commemorating the 100th anniversary of Kate Greenaway's (1846-1901) birth. Kate was an artist and illustrator of numerous children's books during her lifetime. Her designs of young children, flowers, and quaint landscapes are beloved still today. See Leaspun Prints and Leacock.

Kay Dee Designs and Kay Dee Hand Prints, Hope Valley, Rhode Island. Kay Dee Hand Prints was first used in 1952, and Kay Dee Designs in 1990, when they converted to exclusively machine printing. The company produces towels, aprons, pocket mitts, oven mitts, pot holders, hot pads, dish cloths, napkins, bread baskets, placemats, tablecloths, and table runners. We were fortunate to speak to a representative of Kay Dee who was able to provide some insights into the design process of a textile company. The following information is both quoted and paraphrased from that representative, who did not wish to be acknowledged for her assistance.

Kay Dee has a full time design staff under the direction of a Design Director who coordinates styling with both staff and freelance designers. The marketplace today is heavily driven by licensed designs. Images are either selected from these designer portfolios or created in house based on market research. In both the past and the present, it is up to the artist to request that his or her signature appear on the artwork. It gives a certain panache to the image to have it signed by an artist. One of the most prolific designers used by Kay Dee Designs in its early days was Richard Batchelder, who specialized in hand painted scenery. His images were used on framed prints, calendar towels, and linen tea towels. All of his art was hand painted in six colors, then hand color separated for the films necessary to produce the screens used in printing. During the early years, all items produced by Kay Dee Handprints were hand printed. Later, automated machinery was installed and the company changed its name to Kay Dee Designs.

With regard to fabric selection, linen tea towels used to be the mainstay of the industry. Linen is absorbent, lint free, and dries quickly. Linen fell out of favor when "Turkish" towels, or terry towels came into being. During the early years, Kay Dee Handprints purchased its linen toweling from rival Stevens Linen Associates of Dudley, Massachusetts. Later, the linen was purchased from Poland. Today, Kay Dee purchases print blanks and yard goods from a variety of world wide sources including India, China, Taiwan, Vietnam, and Korea.

In its early days, Kay Dee marketed to independent gift shops and was known for hand printed linen calendar towels and tea towels with an especially New England theme. Today, Kay Dee Designs products can be found throughout the country in both the independent trade as well as leading retail vendors. The company continues to screen print in the original facility in Hope Valley, Rhode Island.

We have also found towels by Bestex in the same packaging Kay Dee used ~ the wording and even the address are identical to the Kay Dee Company, although their representative was unaware of any connection. Additional artists we have known to design for Kay Dee include Lois Long and Sewell Jackson.

Kempray, Kemp & Beatley, New York. Textile fabrics in the piece, of cotton, rayon, and combinations thereof; tablecloths, napkins, and kitchen towels. Claim in use since 1940. See also Victory K&B and Vicray.

Kendall, Kendall Co., Walpole, Massachusetts. U.S. patent number 271, 3361. By 1924, successful businessman Henry P. Kendall had merged five of his existing mills into a new corporation, Kendall Mills, Inc. While the company *did* make towels, hospital supplies, and other textiles, they were and still are best known for their Curity diapers, the first pre-folded diaper on the market.

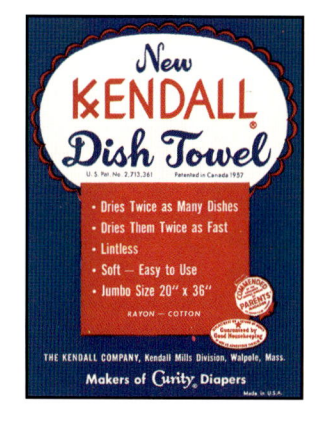

Lady Price, L.B. Price Mercantile Company, St. Louis, Missouri. Produced tablecloths, towels, bath sets, curtains, drapes, bedspreads, sheets, pillowcases, blankets, rugs, furniture slip covers, ironing board covers, and pads. Name was first used in 1953.

Lancaster. See Springmaid.

Leacock Quality Hand Prints, Leacock and Co., Inc., New York. Produced tablecloths, placemats, towels and napkins. Claims in use since 1943. Tablecloths and napkins with the **Colfax** tag were also produced by this very prolific manufacturer. Ivan Bartlett was one designer name produced under the Leacock label. RN#14926.

Leaspun Prints, Leacock and Co., Inc., New York. Claim in use since 1946. See Leacock and Kate Greenaway.

Leda, Leda Lee Design, California. Produced kitchen textiles and tablecloths. U.S. Trademark 233201.

Linen of Queens, The, D. Porthault, Inc. Corporation, New York, New York. Produced household linens, namely towels, sheets, pillowcases, tablecloths, and napkins. First used in 1948 and last registered in 1975. Trademark is now dead.

ML Cloths, Marlene Linens, New York. Produced tablecloths, napkins, and towels. Claim in use since July 1944. Note the absence of the ML logo on some of the tags, yet they are unmistakably Marlene Linens. Numerous ML patterns were produced in Japan after the end of the American occupation in 1952.

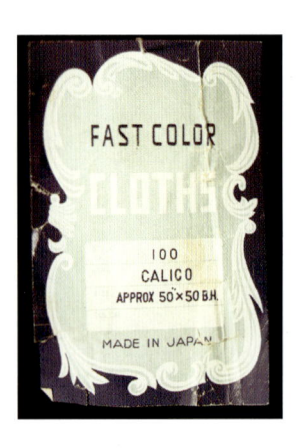

Martex, West Point Stevens Inc., West Point, Georgia. Martex history goes back to 1914. They produced Turkish towels, terry cloths, tablecloths, and napkins. The Martex brand has been owned since 1928 by West Point Stevens. West Point Stevens, with some 190 years of experience, has evolved from three textile giants of the past. Stevens is the company's oldest branch, dating back to 1813 in Massachusetts; Pepperell Manufacturing Company was founded in 1851 in Biddeford, Maine; and West Point Manufacturing Company was incorporated in West Point, Georgia, in 1880. West Point and Pepperell merged in 1965 and Stevens was acquired in 1988. West Point and Stevens now make up the Company name, while the corporate trademark, a stylized griffin, is descended from the old Pepperell dragon trademark.

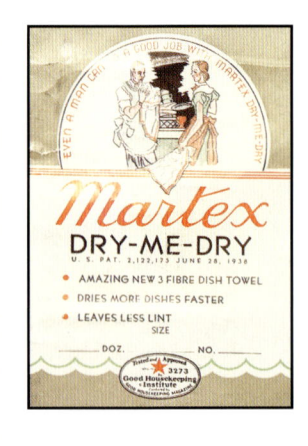

Maytex, Maytex Mills, Inc. Corporation, New York, New York. Housewares, namely vinyl and fabric tablecloths, vinyl and fabric placemats, and kitchen towels. Claim first in use in 1944 and abandoned in 1990.

Macy's Associates, R.H. Macy & Company, Inc. New York. Produced under several labels including Mayflower and Stalwart. The Stalwart name first came into use in 1947 and was renewed in 1971. Trademark is now dead.

Melotex, Herrmann & Jacobs, Inc., New York. For linen, cotton, and cotton and rayon tablecloths and napkins. Claim in use in 1939.

Nileen, Simtex Mills, New York. Produced tablecloths and napkins. First use 1947, renewed 1968. Trademark is dead.

Oppa-tunity, Weil & Durrse, Corporation, New York, New York. Produced tablecloths, napkins, placemats, and towels during the 1940s. See also Wilendur(e), Setting Pretty, and America's Pride.

Parisian Prints. See Joseph Sultan and Sons, JS&S, Exclusive, and Sultan Creations. RN#14788.

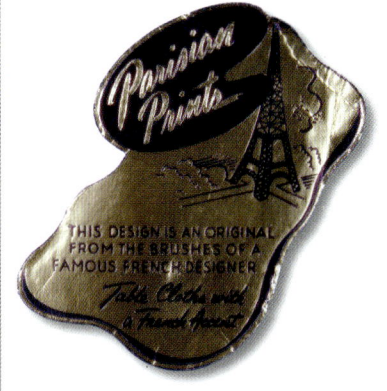

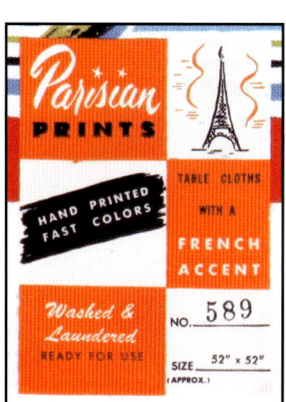

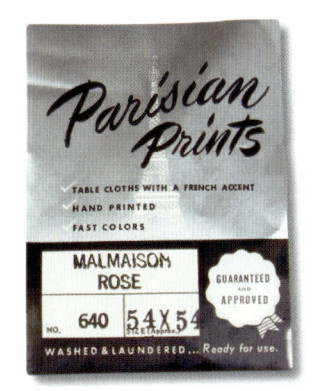

Pennicraft, J.C. Penney Company, Wilmington, Delaware. Tablecloths, card table covers, towels and toweling. Claim in use since September 6, 1940.

145

Pine Tree Linens, Textiles of linen, namely, tablecloths, sheets, napkins, luncheon sets, card table sets, tea sets, breakfast sets, dinner sets, and towels. Claim first in use in 1927 and renewed in 1968. Claim is now dead.

Pride of Flanders, Weil & Durrse, Inc. Corporation, New York. Tablecloths, towels, and toweling of fine Belgian linen. The W&D (Weil and Durrse, aka Wilendur) logo can be found above The Pride of Flanders on numerous tags. Pride of Flanders predates most other lines of Weil and Durrse textiles. See Oppa-tunity, Wilendur, Wilendure, America's Pride, and Setting Pretty.

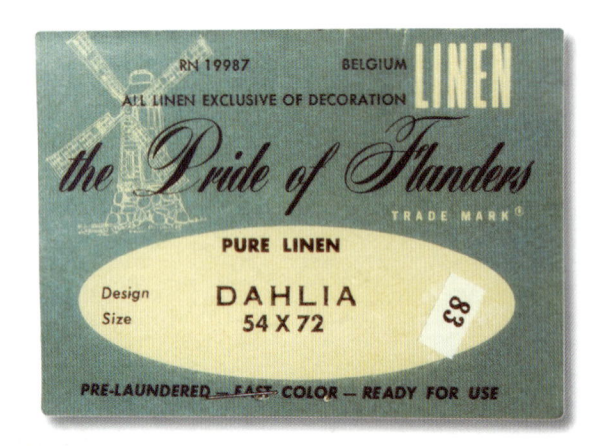

Princess Prints. Part of Broderie Creations line.

Printex, Printex Corporation, New York, New York. Imprinting designs on fabrics of others, said imprinted fabric to be used in the production of articles of wearing apparel, table and bedroom linens, drapes, etc. Claim first in use in 1945 and registered in 1978. Claim is now dead. This is the company founded in 1936 by Vera and her husband.

Prints Charming, Sun Weave Linen Corporation, New York, New York. Importer, wholesaler, manufacturer. Produced tablecloths, napkins, and linens. Claim in use since 1963. Trademark is dead. Also produced Prints Charming E/S, Ann Hathaway Hand Prints, Colorama, and Prints E/S. RN#59216.

146

Queen Anne, Indian Head Mills, Inc., Cordova, Alabama. See Indian Head Mills.

Rosemary High Style Prints, Rosemary Manufacturing, New York, New York. Tablecloths, napkins. First use 1922, renewed in 1983. Note that Rosemary tablecloths often had a little flower logo printed somewhere in the design, identical to the logo found on some Simtex tags. The two companies became loosely connected when they were purchased by parent company J.P. Stevens. **Tablecraft** is another tag name by Rosemary, the claim for which was first in use in the 1930s. See also Stylecraft Prints by Rosemary.

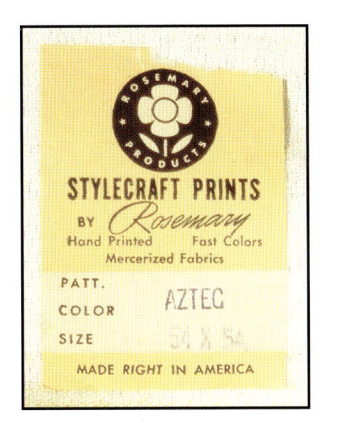

Royal Art, Barth-Guttman Textile Corporation, New York. For piece goods of linen, cotton, rayon, and combinations thereof, tablecloths, napkins, and towels. Claim in use since 1935. Note that the logo is made up of two lions standing and holding the R&A and standing on perfection.

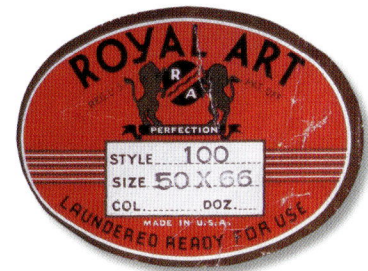

Setting Pretty, Weil & Durrse, Inc. First used 1944, filed with USPTO 1962. Produced tablecloths, napkins, placemats, towels, furniture scarves and throws, toweling, table cover fabrics, and cotton pieced goods. See America's Pride, Oppa-tunity, Setting Pretty, Pride of Flanders, Wilendur(e).

147

Simtex, Simtex Mills, Division of Simmons Company, New York, New York. Table linens, bedspreads, ticking, shirting, decorative and plain piece goods. Claim in use since 1946 and renewed in 1968. Trademark is now dead. Simtex trademarked the name "Matkin" in 1949 for a somewhat elongated rectangular napkin that can also be used as a placemat. They also produced a line of table linens by designer Russell Wright called "Modern."

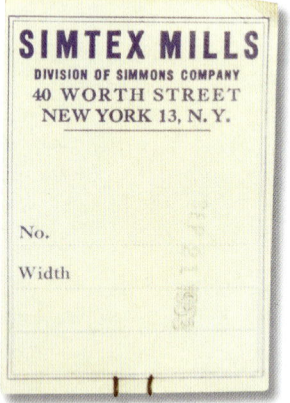

Springmaid, Springs Mills Inc. Fort Mill, South Carolina. Sheets, pillowcases, tablecloths and covers, towels, table napkins, and bedspreads, all cotton, cotton and rayon, and rayon textile fabrics by the piece, by the yard, and in the bolt. Trademark first used in 1926, renewed 1967. The Spring Maiden logo was first in use in 1929 and last renewed in 1969. The company was formed in 1887 by Samuel Elliot White and by 1919 was operating five textile mills in South Carolina. In 1933, the Springs Cotton Mills were created when Elliott White Springs consolidated the five mills into one corporation. Prior to 1940, very few southern mills finished their own textile products. The mill's grey goods (unbleached, unfinished, and uncolored cloth) were sold to northern converters (finishing plants) who in turn bleached, dyed, printed, and finished the grey goods for the consumer market. In 1946, Springmaid eliminated the outside gray goods converter and began producing table linens in addition to their other household textiles. In July 1966, The Springs Cotton Mills and Springmaid, Inc. (selling house) merged to create Spring Mills, Inc. This move was an attempt to coordinate the selling and manufacturing units of the company. Various Springmaid textile lines include Coronet, St Regis, Plaza, Classic, Astor, and Luxuria. They also produced under the names Lancaster and St Regis. None of the Springmaid tablecloths had pattern names; rather they had numbers.

Startex, Startex Mills Corporation, Tucapau, South Carolina. Tablecloths, napkins, kitchen towels, and toweling. Use of the logo **Startex** *without* the star was 1919–December 7, 2002. First use of the logo **Startex** *with* the star was in 1920. Startex was produced at the Spartan Textile Mills, Spartanburg, South Carolina. The Mill opened in 1890. It produced sheeting, bag goods, and broadcloth. After WWII they were know for high quality cotton household fabrics under the brand name "STARTEX." Some commonly found Startex textile lines include Twinkle, Starmont, Garden Prints, Starline, Starbird, and Nu Mode.

State Pride, Belk Stores Services, Inc. Corporation. Charlotte, North Carolina. Tablecloths, napkins, dish towels, aprons, toaster covers. Claim first in use in 1954 and renewed in 1983. Trademark is alive.

Stevens Hand Prints, J.P. Stevens & Co., Inc. Massachusetts. Claim first in use in 1813. J.P. Stevens name has evolved over time; Stevens Fabrics, Stevens Mills, Stevens-Fine Fabrics Since 1813, Stevens Hand Prints. Claim is still in use and registered today under J.P. Stevens of West Point, Georgia. See Martex.

Stylecraft Prints by Rosemary, Rosemary Manufacturing, New York, New York. Tablecloths and napkins. First use 1922. See Rosemary High Style Prints.

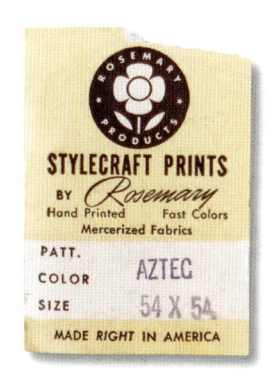

149

Sultan Creations, Joseph Sultan and Sons, New York. See JS&S, Parisian Prints, Exclusive.

Sultana, Appleton Company Corporation, Lowell, Massachusetts. Cotton piece goods. First use 1902, last renewed in 1974.

Sun Glo, Sunweave Linen Corp., 5th Avenue, New York, New York. Importer, wholesaler, manufacturing. RN#15232.

Tanvald, Hermann & Jacobs Corporation, New York, New York. Tablecloths, napkins of linen, cotton, mixtures of silk, cotton, linen, wool, ramie, and mixtures thereof. Claim first in use in 1921 and renewed in 1967. Trademark is now dead.

Taylor, Wellington Sears Company Corporation. See Wellington Fabrics/Wellington Sears.

Thomaston Pedigree, Thomaston Mills, Inc., Thomaston, Georgia. Produced tablecloths, towels and linens. Claim in use since 1940s.

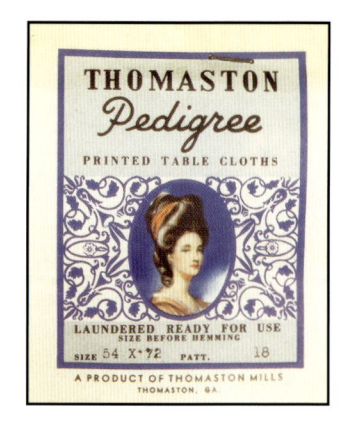

Tiller Brand, Robert A. McFarland, Los Angeles, California. Tablecloths, napkins, towels, and a multitude of other textiles. Claim in use since September 30, 1942.

Town and Country Linen Co., Lakewood, New Jersey. Hedaya Bros. A small horse and buggy logo was often printed on one corner of the design.

Ulster Linen Company, Inc. New York. Ulster Linen Company of New York is the oldest active United States linen company of its kind. A family enterprise since its inception, the company began in Ireland with a mill called The Ulster Weaving Co., Ltd., which was started in the mid 1800s by John Sloan Larmor. John's youngest son, William Hogg Larmor, immigrated to the United States to begin the New York importing company in 1933. At that time, it was called the Ulster Weaving Co., Ltd., as was its Belfast parent company. The company now operates under the name Ulster Linen Company, Inc. The current President and Managing Director is Dever Larmor, a very pleasant gentleman whom we had the pleasure of interviewing. According to Dever, Ulster began manufacturing *printed* tea towels in the 1950s. Other family members carry on the company tradition and are active in its daily operations.

Vera, Scarves by Vera, Inc. Corporation. New York, New York. Table linens, tablecloths, napkins, hand towels, kitchen aprons, place mats. Claim first in use in 1947 and last renewed in 2002. Trademark is alive. In 1946, Vera Salaff Neumann founded the business with her husband, George, and a textile expert named F. Werner Hamm. Her bold, bright designs for scarves, apparel, furnishing fabrics, table linens, and towels were signed only with her first name, Vera. From 1946 to 1967, Vera was a freelance designer for F. Schumacher & Co. Earlier Vera designs feature a ladybug next to her signature; this was used sporadically on her later creations. Some accounts say Vera signed the ladybug to her very first piece ~ others claim it began in the 1950s. The inspiration for her bold, bright and stylized art came from the Hudson River Valley where her studio and home were located.

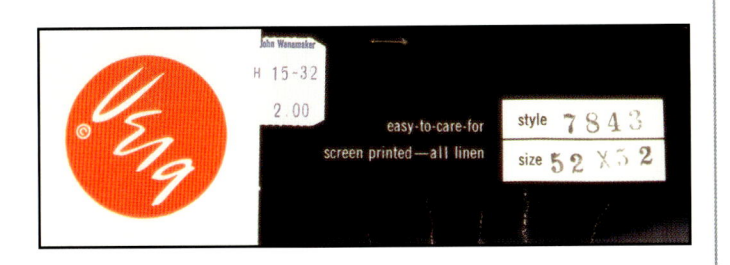

Vicray Hand Prints, Kemp & Beatley, Inc. New York. Textile fabrics in the piece, of cotton, rayon, and combinations thereof; tablecloths, napkins, and kitchen towels. Claim in use since February 27, 1940. RN#16613.

Victory K&B, Kemp & Beatley, Inc. New York. Tablecloths, mat covers, and doilies. Claim in use since 1919. Trademark is now dead.

W&D, Weil & Durrse, Weil & Durrse, Inc. Corporation, New York. Tablecloths, napkins, placemats, towels, toweling, fabrics, and piece goods. See also Genuine Wilendur, Wilendure, America's Pride, Oppa-tunity, Setting Pretty, and The Pride of Flanders.

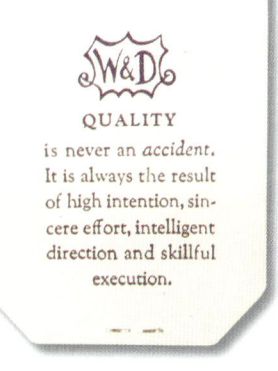

Wellington Fabrics, Wellington Sears Company Corporation, Boston, Massachusetts. Cotton piece goods. Claim in use since 1935, renewed in 1976. RN#16682.

151

Wilendur, Genuine Wilendur, Weil & Durrse, Corporation, New York. Produced tablecloths, napkins, placemats, towels and toweling. Claim in use since October 1939. Filing date October 1939. Trademark abandoned in 1958.

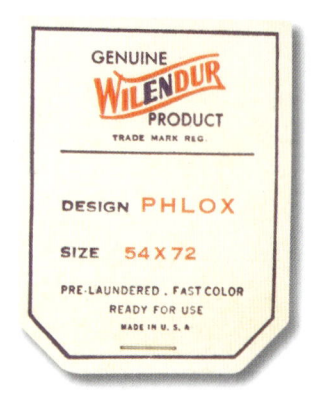

Wilendure, Weil & Durrse Corporation, New York. Produced tablecloths, napkins, placemats, towels, furniture scarves and throws, curtains, drapes, bedspreads and toweling. First use 1958–November 2001.

Yucca Print, An Original, Barth & Dreyfuss, Los Angeles, California. Produced souvenir and western tablecloth/napkin sets on "genuine cactus cloth" during the period 1930-1960. Still producing home furnishing products.

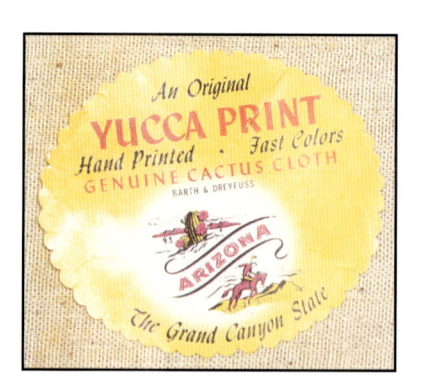

Glossary of Textile Terms

Many of these textile terms and their respective definitions were borrowed from the 1947 edition of the *Callaway Textile Dictionary*. We recommend it as an invaluable reference tool for the textile lover.

Advance Samples. Short lengths, which usually run from six to ten yards in length. They are made up for the coming season, and very often from these samples designs are chosen by the trade. Small swatches of cloth are pasted on cards and distributed to prospective buyers, who thus make their selections.

Affinity. Attraction between two bodies or substances. If a dye takes readily, it is said to have a good affinity for the fiber.

After-Chroming. In dyeing, it is the application of a chrome mordant to material already dyed.

After-Treating. A comprehensive term, usually referring to a process to fix the color on previously dyed material.

Analogous Colors. Commonly known as "neighboring colors" because the colors used have a common property, e.g., bluish green and greenish blue. These colors are one step removed from each other.

Assistants. Substances used as additions to a dye bath to aid in fixing the dyestuff or mordant and to help secure even shading.

Basic Dyes. An important class of dyestuffs. They are salts formed by the combination of dye bases (hence the name) with acids. They will dye wool and silk directly but cotton must be mordanted, usually with tannin. As a class, they give the most brilliant and intense colors of all the dyes, but they have poor fastness properties especially to light and washing. Historically, the basic dyes are the oldest of the synthetic colors, the first being discovered by Perkin in 1856 and known as "Perkins's Mauve."

Bath Ratio. The ratio of the weight of the dye bath to the weight of the material being dyed.

Bleaching. The treatment of textile fibers, yarns, or cloth to destroy the natural coloring matter and leave the material white.

Bleeding. The tendency of a color to come out or run when the material is immersed in water, with consequent staining of this, or other materials in the water.

Block Printing. A method of printing by blocks as apart from roller printing. The material may show a groundwork that has not been printed and, therefore, does not remain white. Printing blocks are made of wood, copper, linoleum, and other materials.

Blotch Printing. The printing of material in order to give it a dyed ground effect. A blotch printed cloth gives the impression that it has been dyed a solid color and discharge printed until close examination reveals that the blotch method was used. The rollers are etched with fine lines to hold the dyestuff for printing so that when the cloth runs through the machine the entire white surface is printed. There will be some absorption on the back of the cloth but it will be almost white.

Body. A term used to describe the feel of fabrics. It indicates that the fabric has considerable bulk or substance, as opposed to a thin or flimsy fabric.

Calendering. One of the most important operations in cloth finishing. The cloth is passed between a series of rollers, usually heated. The pressure of the rollers gives the cloth smoothness and luster.

Chromatic Colors. Those colors that possess hue, such as red, yellow, blue, etc. as distinguished from the achromatic colors, such as white, gray, slate and black.

Cloth. A piece of fabric of a kind, size, and texture adapted for some specific purpose: as a wiping cloth, tablecloth, etc. The word cloth originated from the Fates of Greek mythology. Cloth (Clotho) was one of the three Fates, weaving one web of human destiny.

Color. A particular hue, such as red or blue.

Color Circle. Sometimes known as the chromatic circle, it is the arrangement of the colors of the spectrum in a ring formation, around which each color gradually blends into its related hue.

Colorfast. The term is applied to certain dyed or printed fabrics, especially cotton, to indicate their colors are of sufficient fastness, particularly to light and washing, that no noticeable change in color will take place during the normal life of the material. Correctly speaking, no fabric is absolutely colorfast.

Color Fastness. The ability of a color to meet the standard requirements and specifications of some particular test on yarn or material. Tests include: fastness to washing and laundering, dry cleaning, pressing, ironing, and sunlight, and whether the color will fade or stain.

Color Harmony. The science of using colors in their proper relationships in order to produce pleasing effects.

Color Properties. Colors are considered to have three properties—they are hue, brilliance, and saturation. Hue is the property that distinguishes a color from other colors. Brilliance is that attribute of a color that measures its luminosity, or the degree of lightness or darkness. And saturation is that attribute of chromatic colors which determines their degree of difference from a gray of the same brilliance. If the color is as bright as possible it is known as a saturated or strong color; if it is dull and grayed it is of low saturation.

Color Resist. A chemical, usually a wax preparation, fixed on a cloth in the form of a design which, when the cloth is subsequently dyed, prevents the dyestuff from coloring the area covered by the resist.

Colors. Primary are red, yellow, and blue. Mixing two of the primaries makes secondary colors and mixing two of the secondary colors make tertiary colors. Red and yellow, mixed together, will give orange; yellow and blue give green; blue and red give purple or violet. This second set of colors—orange, green and violet—are the secondary colors. When they, in turn, are mixed together, three colors result that are dull and rather dirty looking: olive, citron and russet.

Converter. The term applied to a man or a firm which buys cotton, rayon, or silk gray goods and sells them in the finished state. The converter gives the instructions as to how the cloth should be finished: dyed, bleached, mercerized, and printed.

Converting. The bleaching, dyeing, printing, or otherwise finishing of a gray cloth to make it into a finished fabric.

Cotton. A soft fibrous substance consisting of the unicellular hairs, which occur, attached to the seeds of various species of plants of the genus Gossypium. Most cotton is creamy white in color but it may be tawny, brownish or reddish. Its cheapness, durability, and versatility make cotton the most important fibrous material of the textile industry.

Developed Dyes. A class of dyestuffs used almost exclusively on cotton. It makes the cotton more colorfast, especially to washing.

Direct Dyes. An important class of dyestuffs distinguished by the common property of dyeing the vegetable fibers in full shades without the aid of mordants. They are comparatively cheap, are readily soluble in water, and are extensively used for dyeing cotton where exceptional fastness properties are not required. Also known as substantive dyes.

Direct Printing. Printing of patterns directly on material from rollers, usually made of copper and engraved to form the pattern on the goods when applied. Also known as Application Printing.

Discharge Printing. A method of printing cloth by the removal of some of the color of the material that has previously been dyed a solid shade. A discharge paste is used, which has the power to destroy coloring matter on the goods. It is applied in the form of a design to the cloth. After the treatment the cloth is then steamed and washed to insure total discharge of the dyestuff and to produce a white discharge print. In a color-discharge print, a color not affected by the discharge paste is added to it.

Dry Goods. Marketing term for textile fabrics: cotton, woolens, rayon, laces, etc.

Dye. A material or matter used for dyeing. Originally, all dyes were of natural origin, but now they are mostly synthetic products.

Dyeing. The process or art of coloring textile or other materials in such a way that the color appears to be a property of the dyed material and not a superficial effect such as that produced by painting. The result of dyeing may be regarded as satisfactory and the material can be truly termed dyed when the color is not easily and quickly removed by actions such as washing, rubbing, light.

Fabric. A collective term applied to cloth no matter how constructed or manufactured and regardless of the kind of fiber from which it is made.

Fastness. The fastness of a dye refers to the ability of the color produced by it to withstand the destructive effect of certain agencies acting upon it, such as washing, light, and ironing.

Fugitive Dyes. Color that are uncertain and tend to bleed or run during a washing process.

Fugitivity. The lack of fastness of dyestuffs to one or more of the various color-destroying agents, such as sunlight, washing, and ironing.

Gray/Grey Goods. Woven or knitted goods just as it leaves the loom or knitting machine and before it has been given any finishing treatment. The term does not imply that the material is gray in color, but rather that it has not been bleached. Also referred to as greige goods.

Hand Blocked. Fabrics printed by hand, generally with the aid of carved wooden blocks.

Hue. One of the three attributes of some colors by virtue of which they differ from the gray of the same brilliance, and in respect to which they fall into classes which may be designated as red, blue, yellow.

Label. In tablecloth and towel collecting, a *sewn in* piece of fabric identifying the manufacturer.

Mangle. A machine for smoothing cloth after washing, such as sheets and tablecloths by roller pressure.

Mercerization. A finishing process extensively used on cotton yarn and cloth, consisting essentially of impregnating the material with a cold, strong, sodium hydroxide solution. The treatment increases the strength and affinity for dyes and, if done under tension, the luster is remarkably increased.

Mercerized Cotton. Cotton yarn or cloth that has been given a mercerization treatment. Usually, only the better quality materials are mercerized.

Metallic Thread. A thread consisting of a core yarn of cotton or silk, around which a filament or strip of metal is twisted.

Mill. A building or collection of buildings with machinery, by which the processes of manufacturing are carried out, such as a cotton mill.

Mordant. Any substance, which, by combining with a dyestuff to form an insoluble compound or lake, serves to produce a fixed color in a textile fiber. Most mordants are metallic salts, although some are acid in nature.

MWT. Abbreviation for Mint with Tag. Original paper tag still affixed to the item.

Natural Dyes. Those derived from various vegetable substances such as roots, wood, bark, lichens, or insects and shellfish.

Nub. A small speck, knot, or lump on a cloth.

Overprint. Colors or designs printed over other colors or motifs. It is resorted to when it is desired to alter shades and tone down certain vivid colors or effects.

Piece Goods. Cloth sold by the yard or some definite cut length.

Printing. The process of producing designs of one or more colors on a fabric. There are several methods, such as roller, block, and screen, and several styles, such as direct, discharge, and resist.

Resist. A chemical substance that will repel or resist dyestuff; a feature of resist printing.

Resist Printing. A style of printing in which a resist is printed on the cloth, after which the cloth is piece dyed, leaving the printed portions unaffected. Usually used for white patterns on colored grounds, although the resist may contain a color different from the ground color.

Roller Printing. A method of printing using engraved metal rollers. There is one roller for each color in the design. The cloth, after printing, is steamed or treated in some way to fix the dye. This method of printing is rapid and comparatively simple. Also called cylinder, calendar, or direct printing.

Run-of-the-Loom. A description for fabric which is shipped to a customer just as it comes off the loom, without inspection and without the elimination of weaving defects.

Run-of-the-Mill. Yarns, fabrics, knit goods, or other textile products which are not inspected, or which do not come up to the standard quality. Usually includes imperfects and seconds.

Sailcloth. A very heavy and strongly made canvas of cotton, linen, or jute.

Screen Printing. A method of fabric printing, somewhat like stenciling, by means of a screen usually made of fine mesh silk cloth. The areas of the screen through which the coloring matter is not to pass are filled with waterproof varnish or other insoluble filler. The color, in the form of a paste, is then forced through the untreated portions of the screen onto the fabric underneath.

Selvage. The lengthwise woven edge of a fabric. To impart additional strength and firmness to the outer edges of the cloth, the ends in the selvage often are of coarser count, with more per inch, than the body of the cloth.

Serging. The overcastting of the raw edges of a cloth.

Silence Cloth. A pad used under a tablecloth to deaden noise and protect the tabletop.

Sizing. The application of a size or starch to warp yarn to increase strength and smoothness and to add weight to the gray goods from the loom.

Slub. A soft, thick uneven place in a yarn. May be a defect or put in the yarn intentionally.

Swatch Book. Also known as pattern book. An annual or seasonal record of a textile mill's production.

Tag. In tablecloth and towel collecting, a piece of paper or sticker attached to the cloth with manufacturer and/or price information.

Taggel. A term coined by the photographer of this book, for those people who get the "tag" and "label" confused.

Turkey Red. A fast, bright scarlet red obtained on cotton by using madder or alizarine on a mordant of aluminum and oil. Formerly of great importance but the dyeing process is long and complicated and it has largely been replaced with colors that are cheaper and easier to apply.

Vat Dyed. An important class of dyes noted for their excellent fastness properties. They are expensive in first cost and in application, but they are widely used on cotton goods, particularly because of their fastness to washing, alkalis, bleaching, and mercerization.

Yellowing. The tendency of certain bleached fabrics to take on a yellowish discoloration when they are stored away. It is usually caused by the incomplete removal of oils and waxes.

Resource Guide

Fine Vintage Linens and Quilts
www.FineVintageLinens.com
A beautiful selection of all types of high quality vintage and antique linens, including many mint condition print tablecloths and tea towels, chenille bedspreads, quilts, vintage bedding and more.

In2VintageCloths
www.rubylane.com/shops/in2vintagecloths
Specializing in mint with paper tag vintage print tablecloths and towels from the 1930s-1960s ~ a wonderful source for the selective collector.

Sharon's Antiques Vintage Fabrics
www.rickrack.com
Superb quality print tablecloths and towels, along with a wide selection of the best in antique and collectible linens, quilts, fabrics, feed sacks, hankies, and more.

Mama Wiskas House of Goodies
www.MamaWiskas.com
Charming and unusual vintage linens from kitsch prints to embroidered heirlooms. Vintage goodies for your retro kitchen and cottage home.

Em's Heart Antique Linens
www.emsheart.com
Fine vintage and antique linens from around the world, including tablecloths, kitchen linens, fine lace, linens for bed, bath and table as well as linen care products.

Easy Street Antiques
www.easystreetantiques.com
Specializing in antique and vintage textiles, including tablecloths and other linens, hankies, scarves, lace, and fabric. Also, antique and vintage jewelry and holiday items.

Gallery of Martin and Lorraine Ryan
www.ryanartduo.com
A glorious glimpse into the life and art of the team known to vintage tablecloth and towels collectors as "The Ryans." Martin and Lorraine have retired from the textile design industry but are still active in the fine art world, and their paintings and watercolors are *extraordinary*. You owe it to yourself to take a peek.

Natural Choices Home Safe Products
www.oxyboost.com
Order Oxy Boost™ and Oxy Prime™ on-line, as well as a host of other extremely effective environmentally safe cleaning products

Magica Rust Remover
www.MagicaRustRemover.com
We buy this stuff in bulk ~ an amazing rust removal product that has so far proven safe on every vintage textile we've tried it on.

Delta Carbona
www.carbona.com
Search for stores in your area that carry the Carbona® Stain Devils™ line of cleaning products, as well as stain removal tricks.

United States Patent and Trademark Office
www.uspto.gov
Search for the trademark history of your tablecloth manufacturer from their database.

Textile Museum of Canada
www.museumfortextiles.on.ca
55 Centre Avenue
Toronto, Ontario, Canada
416/599-5321

The Textile Museum
www.textilemuseum.org
Dedicated to furthering the understanding of mankind's creative achievements in the textile arts.
Washington, DC 20008-4088
202-667-0441

American Textile History Museum
www.athm.org
491 Dutton Street
Lowell, Massachusetts 01854
Phone: 978-441-0400
Fax: 978-441-1412

Lowell National Historical Park – Boott Cotton Mills
The history of America's Industrial Revolution is commemorated in Lowell, Massachusetts. The Boott Cotton Mills Museum, with its operating weave room of 88 power looms, "mill girl" boardinghouses, the Suffolk Mill Turbine Exhibit, and guided tours, tells the story of the transition from farm to factory, chronicles immigrant and labor history, and traces industrial technology. The park includes textile mills, worker housing, 5.6 miles of canals, and 19th-century commercial buildings.
67 Kirk Street
Lowell, Massachusetts 01852

Smithsonian Institution Research Information System (SIRIS)
PO Box 37012 MRC 154
Washington, DC 20013-7012
Phone: 202-357-2240
Fax: 202-786-2866

Genealogical Storage Products
www.genealogicalstorageproducts.com
9401 Northeast Drive
Fredericksburg, Virginia 22408
Phone: 800/634-0491
Fax: 800/947-8814
A reasonably priced source of acid free tissue.

Bibliography

Barineau, Yvonne, and Erin Henderson. *Colorful Tablecloths 1930s-1960s: Threads of the Past*. Atglen, PA: Schiffer Publishing, Ltd., 2004.

Bendure, Zelma, and Gladys Pfeiffer. *America's Fabrics–Origin and History, Manufacture, Characteristics and Use*. New York, New York: The Macmillian Company, 1947.

Bonneville, Francoise de. *The Book of Fine Linen*. Paris, France: Flammarion, 2001.

Bosker, Gideon, Michele Mancini, and John Gramstad. *Fabulous Fabrics of the 50s*. San Francisco, California: Chronicle Books, 1992.

Carmichael, W.L., George E. Linton, and Isaac Price. *Callaway Textile Dictionary*. La Grange, Georgia: Callaway Mills, 1947.

Collins, Herbert Ridgeway. *Threads of History: Americana Recorded on Cloth, 1775 to the Present*. Washington, D.C.: Smithsonian Institution Press, 1979.

Gallery of Martin and Lorraine Ryan, http://www.ryanartduo.com/

Halberstam, David. *The Fifties*. New York, New York: Villard Books, 1993.

Kirkham, Pat. *Women Designers in the USA 1900-2000*. Yale University Press, 2000.

Linton, George E. *The Modern Textile Dictionary*. New York, New York: Duell, Sloan and Pearce–Little Brown and Company, 1954.

Meller, Susan, and Joost Elffers. *Textile Designs–Two Hundred Years of European and American Patterns Organized by Motif, Style, Color, Layout and Period*. New York, New York: Harry N. Abrams, Inc. 1991.

Nantucket Historical Association, http://www.nha.org

Peel, Lucy, and Polly Powell. *Fifties and Sixties Style*. Seacaucus, New Jersey: Chartwell Books, 1988.

Pettus, Louise. *The Springs Story–Our First Hundred Years*. Fort Mill, South Carolina: Springs Industries, Inc. 1987.

Scofield, Elizabeth, and Peggy Zalamea. *Fun Linens and Handkerchiefs of the 20th Century*. Atglen, Pennsylvania: Schiffer Publishing Ltd., 2002.

Smithsonian National Museum of American History web site, http://americanhistory.si.edu/house/yourvisit/victorygarden.asp

Temple, Mary Beth. *Rescuing Vintage Textiles*. Haworth, New Jersey: St. Johann Press, 2000.

Trestain, Eileen Jahnke. *Dating Fabrics–A Color Guide 1800-1960*. Paducah, Kentucky: American Quilter's Society, 1998.

Ulster Linen Company, Inc. New York, http://www.pagelinx.com/ulsterlinen/index.htm

University of New England Art Gallery, http://www.une.edu/artgallery/

Wallis, Melanie. *Village Care of New York, Senior Advocate*. August 1993, page 7.

Zito, Vinzento. *Dogs*. New York, New York: Wohlfahet Studios, 1937.

Index

A&S, 136
A.R. Rosenthal, Inc., 136
Abraham & Straus, 136
All Time Towels, 54
America's Pride, 14, 136, 145
Ann Hathaway Hand Prints, 146
Aristocraft, 136
Artmart Decropak, 52
Aunt Martha, 33
Barth & Dreyfuss, 77, 101
Barth-Guttman Textile Corporation, 147
Bartlett, Ivan, 97, 143
Batchelder, Richard, 142
Bates/Bates Manufacturing Company, 136
Beals, Victor, 90
Belcrest Linens/Belcrest Prints, 75, 115, 136
Belk Stores Services, Inc., Corporation, 149
Berhard Ulmann Co., Inc., 137
Bestex Hand Prints, 94, 136, 143
Bloomcraft, 89
Bloomingdale's/Bloomingdale Brothers, Inc., 136
Bogdanovich, Sergei, 5, 9, 15, 16, 98, 112
Bogdanovich, Tamara, 5, 9, 15, 16, 89, 112
Boott Mills, 81, 136
Briard, Georges, 96
Broderie Creations, 7, 18, 24, 39, 42, 43, 44, 56, 57, 58, 59, 70, 102, 113, 128, 136
Bucilla Hand Prints/Bucilla Needlecraft, 31, 57, 67, 81, 137
Burlington Industries, Inc./Burlington Mills Corporation, 137
Bur-Mil, 137
Bush, George, 138
Cage, John, 91
Calaprint, 137
Calcot Hand Prints, 70
California Hand Prints, 17, 22, 137
California Piece Dye Works, 138
Callaway Mills Corporation, 137
Cannon/Cannon Mills, Co./Cannon Rapidry, 8, 80, 81, 138, 140
Cannon, Charles, 138
Cannon, James William, 138
Carol Creation, 78

Century Loom, 138
Charm Prints, 138
CHP, 137
Cohama, 138
Cohn-Hall-Marx Co., 138
Colfax, 143
Colonial Hand Prints, 138
Color Craft, 79
Colorama, 146
Color-fornia, 138
Cugat, Xavier, 96
Days-of-the-Week towels (DOW), 32, 33, 34
D. Porthault, Inc., Corporation, 144
Decorative Linens Manufacturing, 65
Dewan, 138
Dorn, Marion Victoria, 99
Dry-Me-Dry, 5, 45, 48, 109, 111
Dunmoy, 138
Dutch Girl, 90
E&W, 138
E/S Colorama, 139, 146
Eaton/Eaton's Department Stores, 7
Edmond Dewan and Company, 91, 95, 138
Edson, Inc., Co., 139
Edsonart, 139
Ely, Frank, 138
Ely, Walker and Company, 138
Erinore, 104
Everfast/Everfast Fabrics, Inc., 139
Excello, 82
Exclusive, 139, 142
Eye Appeal, 15
F. Schumacher & Co., 92, 151
F. Werner Hamm, 151
F.W. Woolworth Co., Corporation, 141
Falflax, 139
Fallani & Cohn, Inc., 86, 87, 90, 91, 95, 139
Falspun, 139
Faltex, 139
Fashion Manor, 139
Fiatelle Co., 139
Fieldcrest/Fieldcrest-Cannon, Inc., 138, 140
First Lady, 140
Forester, Rosalie, 59, 60
Foxcroft, 138
Fruit of the Loom, Inc., 17, 40, 140
Fruitana, 140
Garden Prints, 141

Garden State Creation/House of Prints/Table Toppers, 141
Gilbrae, 138
Gribbon Company, Inc. Corporation, 141
Gribbon's, 82, 141
GW/Grossman & Weissman, Inc., 59, 60
GW Litho Craft, 24
GW Prismacolor, 59
GW Textile Product, 8, 42
Hadson, 63
Hanson, 81, 82
Happy Home, 141
Hardy Craft, 11, 105, 141
Hardy Tex, 141
Harmony House, 141
Hawaiian Hand Prints, 137
Hedaya Importing Co., 141
Herrman & Jacobs Corporation, Inc., 145
Hico Master Prints, 141
Hollywood Hand Print, 141
Horse and Buggy logo, 9
Huck Towel, 28, 29
Huckaback, 28
Imperial, 64
Indian Head Mills, Inc., 142, 147
J. Spencer Love, 137
J.C. Penney's Co., 54
J. P. Stevens & Co., Inc., 149
Jackson, Sewell, 143
James G. Hardy and Co., Corporation, 141
JBM Original Creation, 55, 96
Joseph Sultan and Sons, 43, 46, 104, 142, 145
JS&S, 43, 46, 105, 142, 145
Kannopolis, 138
Kate Greenaway, 99, 142, 144
Kay Dee Company/Kay Dee Designs/Kay Dee Hand Prints, 91, 94, 121, 142, 143
Keefe, Tammis, 86, 87, 88, 139
Kemp & Beatley, Inc., 143
Kempray, 143
Kendall, 143
Kimball, 86, 88
Knight, Benjamin and Robert, 140
L.B. Price Mercantile Company, 143
La Rhumba, 138
Lady Christina Household Linens, 65

Lady Price, 12, 143
Ladybug logo, 92, 151
Lamb, Tom, 63, 96, 141
Lancaster, 143
Larmor, Dever, 104, 150
Larmor, John Sloan, 150
Larmor, William Hogg, 150
Leacock, 13, 25, 26, 72, 97, 99, 100, 106, 107, 110, 111, 115, 143
Leaspun, 99, 143, 144
Leda, 25, 144
Leda Lee Design, 144
Linen of Queens, The, 144
Long, Lois, 75, 91, 143
Lorraine, 33
Lowell National Historic Park-Boott Cotton Mills, 81, 157
Lustre Dry, 101
Macy's Associates, 145
Madsen, John, 15, 23, 25, 26, 41
Marlene Linens (ML), 144
Marshall Fields and Company, 140
Martex, 45, 48, 83, 109, 111, 114, 144
Martha, 106, 107
Marvel Linen Corporation, 140
Mastercraft Hand Prints, 13
Mayflower, 145
Maytex Mills, Inc. Corporation, 144
Meir, C.P., 84
Melotex, 145
Mercantile Stores, Company, Inc., 140
Miami Originals of Miami, 120
ML Cloths, 144
Morgan Jones, 78, 80
Nileen, 145
Oppa-tunity, 145
Orlana, 42
Orr, Ann, 45
Overtex, 53
Paragon Needlecraft Company/Paragon Prints, 30, 31, 53, 51, 63, 73
Parisian Prints, 101, 104, 114, 117, 124, 145
Pennicraft, 145
Pepperell Manufacturing Company, 144
Pillowtex Corporation, 138
Pine Tree Linens, 146

Pride of Flanders, The, 10, 11, 14, 22, 23, 38, 146
Princess Prints, 146
Printex, 146
Prints Charming, 146
Prints E/S, 146
Pritchard, Pat, 88, 89
Progress, 32
P&S Creations, 49, 51, 62, 72
Quality Prints, 67, 143
Queen Anne, 147
Rapidry, 79
Rey Aine, 71
R.H. Macy & Company, Inc., 145
Rosemary High Style Prints, 147
Rosemary Manufacturing, 147
Royal Art, 147
Royal Doulton, 59, 60, 61
Royal Terry, 77
Ryan, Martin and Lorraine, 95, 139
Ryans, The, 95, 139
Sara Jane Prints, 40, 57
Sarg, Mary, 90, 91, 138
Sarg, Tony, 74, 90, 91
Sears Roebuck & Co., 141
Setting Pretty, 145, 147
Simmons Company, 148
Simtex/Simtex Mills, 78, 148
Smith, Edward C., 94
Society Creations, 64, 125
Spring Maid, The, 67, 148
Springmaid, Inc. 67, 68, 69, 148
Springs Cotton Mills, 148
Springs, Elliot White, 148
Springs Mills, Inc., 148
Stalwart, 145
Startex, 10, 13, 25, 26, 36, 37, 38, 40, 123, 149
State Pride, 149
Stevens Hand Prints, 9, 144, 149
Stevens Mills, 149
Stylecraft Prints by Rosemary, 147, 149
Styled by Dewan, 38
Sultan Creations, 145, 150
Sultana, 150
Sun Glo, 110, 11, 121, 150
Sun Weave Linen Corporation, 146

Superior Hand Print of Los Angeles, 113
Superior Quality, 40, 62
Tablecraft, 147
Tanvald, 150
Taylor, 150
Technicolor Print, 7
The Textile Museum, 156
Thomas, Peg, 87
Thomaston Mills, Inc., 150
Thomaston Pedigree, 150
Tiller Brand, 150
Tobin, Sporn, Glaser, 32
Townhouse Kitchen Decoratives, 88, 89, 91
Town & Country Linen Company, 9, 74, 103, 121, 123, 150
Travis, Luther, 89, 90, 139
Tropical Hand Prints, 137
Tucker, Richard, 93
Twinkle, 78
Ulster Linen Company, Inc., 104, 150
Ulster Weaving Co., Ltd., 150
Union Oilcloth Company, 138
Vera/Vera Salaff Neumann, 92, 93, 151
Vicray Hand Prints, 151
Victory K&B, 21, 37, 103, 151
Vogart, 33
W&D, 151
Walker, David Davis, 138
Weil & Durrse, Inc., 38, 151
Wellington Fabrics, 151
Wellington Sears Company, Corporation, 45, 118, 150
West Point Manufacturing Company, 144, 149
Westpoint Stevens, Inc., 144, 149
White, Samuel Elliot, 148
Wilendur, 5, 6, 7, 9, 10, 11, 12, 14, 15, 16, 17, 25, 26, 37, 41, 98, 103, 106, 114, 152
Wilendure, 25, 103, 145
Wilson, Carrie, 95, 138
Wonder Dri, 5
Yucca Print, 119, 152
Zito, Virginia, 85
Zito, Vinzento, 85, 86